EMERGENCY AND INTENSIVE CARE MEDICINE

HOSPITAL EMERGENCY DEPARTMENTS

BACKGROUND, ISSUES, AND TRENDS

EMERGENCY AND INTENSIVE CARE MEDICINE

Additional books in this series can be found on Nova's website
under the Series tab.

Additional e-books in this series can be found on Nova's website
under the e-book tab.

EMERGENCY AND INTENSIVE CARE MEDICINE

HOSPITAL EMERGENCY DEPARTMENTS

BACKGROUND, ISSUES, AND TRENDS

DANIEL T. LEE
EDITOR

nova publishers
New York

NOTICE TO THE READER

Library of Congress Cataloging-in-Publication Data

ISBN: 978-1-63482-170-4

Published by Nova Science Publishers, Inc. † New York

CONTENTS

PREFACE

This book describes EDs and the role they play in the health care delivery system. It also discusses the federal role and interest in supporting emergency care.

Chapter 1 – Hospital-based Emergency Departments (EDs) are required to stabilize patients with emergent conditions regardless of the patients' ability to pay as a requirement of the Emergency Medical Treatment and Active Labor Act (EMTALA). Given this requirement, EDs play an important part in the health care safety net by serving the uninsured, the underserved, and those enrolled in Medicaid. Open 24 hours a day, EDs provide emergency care, urgent care, primary care, and behavioral health care services in communities where these services are unavailable or unavailable after hours. EDs also play a key role during emergencies, such as natural disasters.

Some EDs are challenged to provide effective care. For example, EDs provide a disproportionate amount of health care to the U.S. population, in general, and to the safety net population, in particular. Specifically, while 4% of all U.S. physicians are ED physicians, they are the treating physicians in 28% of all acute care visits. Some EDs face financial challenges. ED services are costly both to payers, because services provided in an ED are more costly than those provided in community-based settings, and to hospitals, because operating an ED has high fixed costs and because if patients enter with an emergent condition, hospitals are required by EMTALA to stabilize the patient regardless of the patient's ability to pay.

As providers of uncompensated safety net care, some EDs are crowded, in part because hospitals lack staff or inpatient beds to transfer patients from the ED, and in part because of the large number of patients who seek care in the ED because care is unavailable or inaccessible in the community. Crowded conditions have resulted in some patients experiencing long wait times, which, at times, delays access to care and results in worse health outcomes. In addition, hospitals, particularly those in urban areas, are regularly diverting ambulances because they are too crowded to accept new patients.

This report describes EDs and the role they play in the health care delivery system. It also discusses the federal role and interest in supporting emergency care. The federal government is the largest payer for overall health care, through the Medicare and Medicaid programs. Also, the federal government has made investments in emergency preparedness, programs and efforts that support the health care safety net, and health care access in general. Given these investments, Congress may be interested in EDs because a well-functioning ED system is necessary to provide surge capacity in an emergency. The function of the ED system, in turn, reflects its surrounding community's access to health care services; therefore, understanding the use of EDs, evaluating whether such use is appropriate, and examining strategies employed to reduce inappropriate use may all be of policy interest.

This report discusses three commonly identified and interrelated challenges that EDs face: (1) crowding in EDs, (2) providing repeat care to a subset of patients who are frequent users, and (3) providing care to a large population who have behavioral health conditions when an ED lacks the appropriate resources to provide such treatment. Finally, this report concludes with some policy options that Congress might consider to improve ED functioning and reduce payer costs. This report focuses on EDs that are available to the general population; as such, it does not include EDs operated by the Departments of Defense or Veterans Affairs or those operated by the Indian Health Service.

Chapter 2 – The Emergency Medical Treatment and Active Labor Act (EMTALA) ensures universal access to emergency medical care at all Medicare participating hospitals with emergency departments. Under EMTALA, any person who seeks emergency medical care at a covered facility, regardless of ability to pay, immigration status, or any other characteristic, is guaranteed an appropriate screening exam and stabilization treatment before transfer or discharge. Failure to abide by these requirements can subject hospitals or physicians to civil monetary sanctions or exclusion from Medicare. Hospitals, but not physicians, may also be sued by private individuals who suffer personal injuries as a result of a violation of EMTALA.

A dispute over the interpretation of the statute has recently arisen in the context of the application of EMTALA to individuals who come to a hospital emergency room and are subsequently admitted to the hospital as inpatients. Regulations promulgated by the Centers for Medicare and Medicaid Services

(CMS) have taken the position that a hospital's EMTALA obligations end once an individual is admitted as an inpatient. However, in *Moses v. Providence Hospital*, the United States Court of Appeals for the Sixth Circuit held that, despite these regulations, transferring or discharging an *inpatient* without stabilizing an emergency medical condition could still constitute a violation of EMTALA. Consequently, a hospital's obligations to inpatients under EMTALA may be modulated by the *Moses* decision if the hospital happens to be located in the Sixth Circuit's jurisdiction (Kentucky, Michigan, Ohio, and Tennessee).

In December of 2010, CMS solicited comments on whether CMS's inpatient regulations should be revisited. The solicited comments may provide specific examples of individuals' treatment after being admitted from the emergency room, which may be of interest to both agency officials and legislators.

Chapter 3 – Emergency departments (EDs) provide a significant source of medical care in the United States, with over 131 million total ED visits occurring in 2011. Over the past decade, the increase in ED utilization has outpaced growth of the general population, despite a national decline in the total number of ED facilities. In 2009, approximately half of all hospital inpatient admissions originated in the ED. In particular, EDs were the primary portal of entry for hospital admission for uninsured and publicly insured patients (privately insured patients were more likely to be directly admitted to the hospital from a doctor's office or clinic).

ED utilization reflects the greater health needs of the surrounding community and may provide the only readily available care for individuals who cannot obtain care elsewhere. Many ED visits are "resource sensitive" and potentially preventable, meaning that access to high-quality, community-based health care can prevent the need for a portion of ED visits.

This HCUP Statistical Brief presents data on ED visits in the United States in 2011. Patient and hospital characteristics for two types of ED visits are provided: ED visits with admission to the same hospital and ED visits resulting in discharge, which includes patients who were stabilized in the ED and then discharged home, transferred to another hospital, or any other disposition. The most frequent conditions treated by patient age group also are presented for both types of ED visits. All differences between estimates noted in the text are statistically significant at the .0005 level or better.

Chapter 4 – There has been an overall increase in emergency department (ED) visits over the past two decades. However, ED visits for specific conditions have shown varying patterns, and visits for some conditions have decreased in recent years.

There are a number of factors that may affect both positive and negative trends in growth for condition-specific ED visits. Some of those factors are personal, such as an individual's specific health condition. Other factors are related to the community where the individual lives—for example, the availability of health care options.

Changes in health care are reflected in ED use. For example, with improved care coordination some conditions may now be more effectively managed in the outpatient setting, which reduces the need for the acute care provided by EDs. Updated information about trends in ED use over time reveals the changing needs of individuals in the community and emerging transformations in health care policies.

This HCUP Statistical Brief presents data on changes in overall ED visits from 2006 through 2011. ED visit rates are reported by patient demographic characteristics and tracked by patient age. Changes in ED visit rates for the most common conditions and the conditions with the greatest changes also are provided. Changes in rates are considered statistically significant if the p-value is 0.05 or less.

Chapter 5 – Emergency rooms (ERs) are intended to provide care for acute and life-threatening medical conditions for people of all ages, but use is highest among older adults and young children. In 2012, 18% of children aged 0–17 years visited the ER at least once in the past year. Rising health care costs make it important to understand the reasons that families with children seek ER care, rather than less expensive office-based or outpatient care. Families visiting the ER at night or on weekends may have different characteristics or reasons for using the ER than those who visit during the day. Previous research among adults found that the majority visited the ER because "only a hospital could help," or the "doctor's office [was] not open." This report provides comparable statistics on reasons for children's ER use.

In: Hospital Emergency Departments
Editor: Daniel T. Lee
ISBN: 978-1-63482-170-4

Chapter 1

HOSPITAL-BASED EMERGENCY DEPARTMENTS: BACKGROUND AND POLICY CONSIDERATIONS*

Elayne J. Heisler and Nancy Leigh Tyler

SUMMARY

Hospital-based Emergency Departments (EDs) are required to stabilize patients with emergent conditions regardless of the patients' ability to pay as a requirement of the Emergency Medical Treatment and Active Labor Act (EMTALA). Given this requirement, EDs play an important part in the health care safety net by serving the uninsured, the underserved, and those enrolled in Medicaid. Open 24 hours a day, EDs provide emergency care, urgent care, primary care, and behavioral health care services in communities where these services are unavailable or unavailable after hours. EDs also play a key role during emergencies, such as natural disasters.

Some EDs are challenged to provide effective care. For example, EDs provide a disproportionate amount of health care to the U.S. population, in general, and to the safety net population, in particular. Specifically, while 4% of all U.S. physicians are ED physicians, they are the treating physicians in 28% of all acute care visits. Some EDs face

* This is an edited, reformatted and augmented version of a Congressional Research Service publication R43812, prepared for Members and Committees of Congress, dated December 8, 2014.

financial challenges. ED services are costly both to payers, because services provided in an ED are more costly than those provided in community-based settings, and to hospitals, because operating an ED has high fixed costs and because if patients enter with an emergent condition, hospitals are required by EMTALA to stabilize the patient regardless of the patient's ability to pay.

As providers of uncompensated safety net care, some EDs are crowded, in part because hospitals lack staff or inpatient beds to transfer patients from the ED, and in part because of the large number of patients who seek care in the ED because care is unavailable or inaccessible in the community. Crowded conditions have resulted in some patients experiencing long wait times, which, at times, delays access to care and results in worse health outcomes. In addition, hospitals, particularly those in urban areas, are regularly diverting ambulances because they are too crowded to accept new patients.

This report describes EDs and the role they play in the health care delivery system. It also discusses the federal role and interest in supporting emergency care. The federal government is the largest payer for overall health care, through the Medicare and Medicaid programs. Also, the federal government has made investments in emergency preparedness, programs and efforts that support the health care safety net, and health care access in general. Given these investments, Congress may be interested in EDs because a well-functioning ED system is necessary to provide surge capacity in an emergency. The function of the ED system, in turn, reflects its surrounding community's access to health care services; therefore, understanding the use of EDs, evaluating whether such use is appropriate, and examining strategies employed to reduce inappropriate use may all be of policy interest.

This report discusses three commonly identified and interrelated challenges that EDs face: (1) crowding in EDs, (2) providing repeat care to a subset of patients who are frequent users, and (3) providing care to a large population who have behavioral health conditions when an ED lacks the appropriate resources to provide such treatment. Finally, this report concludes with some policy options that Congress might consider to improve ED functioning and reduce payer costs. This report focuses on EDs that are available to the general population; as such, it does not include EDs operated by the Departments of Defense or Veterans Affairs or those operated by the Indian Health Service.

INTRODUCTION

Emergency departments (EDs) play an important public health role during emergencies and on a regular basis by providing access to emergency care to all patients regardless of their ability to pay (see *Text Box 1*).[1] Although the original intent of EDs was to provide emergency care, this role has expanded, as patients often seek care in an ED when services are unavailable or inaccessible in the community. Federal law guarantees access to emergency services under the Emergency Medical Treatment and Active Labor Act (EMTALA), which requires that hospitals screen all patients who enter their ED and stabilize those with emergent conditions regardless of the patients' insurance status. Hospitals that fail to do so can be excluded from the Medicare program.[2] As a consequence of EMTALA, hospitals with EDs must provide emergency care, which may be un- or under compensated (i.e., the hospital may not recover any or all of the cost of treatment). Specifically, more than 40% of all ED visits are for individuals who are uninsured or enrolled in Medicaid, two types of patients where hospitals provide care that is un- or under compensated.[3]

Introduction

Emergency departments (EDs) play an important public health role during emergencies and on a regular basis by providing access to emergency care to all patients regardless of their ability to pay (see *Text Box 1*).[1] Although the original intent of EDs was to provide emergency care, this role has expanded, as patients often seek care in an ED when services are unavailable or inaccessible in the community. Federal law guarantees access to emergency services under the Emergency Medical Treatment and Active Labor Act (EMTALA), which requires that hospitals screen all patients who enter their ED and stabilize those with emergent conditions regardless of the patients' insurance status. Hospitals that fail to do so can be excluded from the Medicare program.[2] As a consequence of EMTALA, hospitals with EDs must provide emergency care, which may be un- or under compensated (i.e., the hospital may not recover any or all of the cost of treatment). Specifically, more than 40% of all ED visits are for individuals who are uninsured or enrolled in Medicaid, two types of patients where hospitals provide care that is un- or under compensated.[3]

EDs provide a disproportionate amount of health care to the U.S. population. Specifically, the 4% of physicians who staff EDs are the treating physician in 28% of all acute care visits,[4] and these visits disproportionately involve patients with more dangerous or worrisome symptoms, such as chest pain, respiratory complaints, and abdominal pain.[5] From 1992 to 2012, the number of ED visits grew faster than the U.S. population. This occurred for a number of reasons, including the immediate access to diagnostic resources that EDs provide and community-level declines in access to primary or behavioral health care, which have occurred at the same time as population-level increases in rates of chronic conditions (see *Table 1).*[6]

Table 1. Emergency Department Visits

Year	ED Visits (millions)	ED Visits (per 1,000 population)
1992	90.8	356
2002	110.0	382
2012	133.2	424

Source: American Hospital Association, TrendWatch Chartbook 2014, Table 3.3 Emergency Department Visits, Emergency Department Visits per 1,000 and Number of Emergency Departments, 1992-2012, http://www.aha.org/research/reports/tw/chartbook/index.shtml.

EDs also provide a significant amount of care to safety net populations. EDs handle two-thirds of acute care visits for the uninsured and one half of the acute care visits of people enrolled in Medicaid or the State Children's Health Insurance Program (CHIP).[7] In some cases, EDs are the appropriate site for care, but, in other cases, non-emergent patients seek care in an ED because they lack an alternative source of care. This occurs for a number of reasons, including the patients' insurance status, their relationship to a regular provider, and their ability to secure a timely appointment with that provider.[8] The use of EDs to provide nonemergency care can be costly to payers because services provided in an ED are generally more expensive than those provided in community-based settings. ED services are more expensive, because, for example, EDs have higher fixed costs (in terms of space and staffing), its physicians may order additional tests or laboratory work, and because hospital charges are generally higher than those charged by physician's offices.[9]

As a result of increased ED use and declining financial support for providing this volume of care, the Institute of Medicine, in a series of three reports published in 2006, declared that ED care was "at a breaking point."[10] Subsequent work by the Government Accountability Office (GAO) confirmed that these challenges persisted and found that EDs were crowded, that they diverted ambulances because they were unable to accept new patients, and that patients often experienced long waits for care.[11] Although recent changes to health care delivery and financing (e.g., the growth of retail clinics[12] and increases in the number of people who are insured because of the Patient Protection and Affordable Care Act)[13] may improve ED operations for some hospitals, EDs—particularly those in urban area—remain crowded.[14] It is also possible that some policy changes may have unintended consequences increasing ED use or further straining ED finances.[15]

The federal government is interested in the availability of ED services and their appropriate use for several reasons, including its role as a payer of health care services, its role in supporting emergency preparedness, and its role in supporting the health care safety net. The federal government is the largest health care payer, through the Medicare and Medicaid programs,[16] and as such, the availability, use, and costs of ED services may be of interest to policy makers.[17] Also, the federal government has made investments in emergency preparedness,[18] programs and efforts that support the health care safety net, and efforts that support health care access in general.[19] Given these investments, Congress may be interested in EDs because a well-functioning ED system is necessary to provide surge capacity in an emergency. The function of the ED system, in turn, often reflects its surrounding community's access to health care services; therefore, understanding the use of EDs, evaluating whether such use is appropriate, and examining strategies employed to reduce inappropriate use may all be of policy interest.

This report describes EDs, the role they play in the health care delivery system, and current federal involvement in supporting EDs.[20] It then discusses the causes and consequences of three commonly identified and interrelated challenges that EDs face: (1) crowding, (2) providing repeat care to a subset of patients who are frequent users, and (3) providing care to a large population who have behavioral health conditions when an ED lacks the appropriate resources to provide such treatment. The report concludes with policy options that Congress may consider to potentially improve ED functioning and reduce payer costs.

EDs and Health Care Delivery

EDs play a role in the U.S. health care system that has expanded beyond their original purpose of providing emergency care. EDs are increasingly relied upon to fill gaps in available care by providing after-hours care, by providing care to the safety net population, and by providing behavioral health care when such care is not otherwise available. EDs are also increasingly providing types of care that have traditionally been provided by primary care providers (PCPs), such as conducting diagnostic testing (e.g., blood testing) and coordinating chronic care (e.g., care to manage a chronic disease such as diabetes). The role of an ED within a hospital has also changed, as EDs, instead of PCPs, increasingly drive hospital admissions, an important source of hospital revenue. This section provides an overview of the expanded role of EDs. All EDs provide similar types of care, but they may see different patient populations depending on their location (e.g., rural areas versus urban areas), and the services offered, as some EDs may offer specialized services such as trauma or burn care.[21]

EDs generally provide three types of care: (1) emergency care, (2) unscheduled urgent care, and (3) safety net care (see *Text Box 2*). Emergency care is the primary and original mission of EDs. Unscheduled urgent care may be used to treat an acute problem or the acute exacerbation of a chronic health problem. EDs may provide safety net care because patients have financial or other barriers that prevent them from accessing care from other components of the health care system.[22] Primary and behavioral health care are often provided in an ED as a result of either unscheduled urgent care or as part of an ED's safety net function. In both these cases, it is not optimal to provide these services in an ED.

Text Box 2: Three Types of Care Commonly Provided by Emergency Departments

1. *Emergency Care*: the treatment of seriously ill or injured patients who requirement immediate stabilizing treatment.
2. *Unscheduled urgent care*: care provided for acute problems or acute exacerbation of chronic problems, generally because there is inadequate capacity in other parts of health care system.
3. *Safety net care*: care provided to vulnerable populations who experience barriers that prevent them from accessing care from other parts of the health care system. As a consequence, this population uses EDs regularly for care, typically because cost or barriers to access prevent them from obtaining care in other settings.

Source: Brent R. Asplin et al., "A Conceptual Model of Emergency Department Crowding," Annals of Emergency Medicine, vol. 42, no. 2 (August 2003), pp. 173-180 and Institute of Medicine of the National Academies, Hospital-Based Emergency Care: At the Breaking Point (Washington, DC: National Academies Press, 2006).

EDs Fill Gaps in Available Care

ED use reflects the health needs of the surrounding community and the gaps in care available because EDs provide care to those with few alternate options. Given this, some ED visits may be considered "resource sensitive" and preventable if appropriate community-based resources are available.[23] Community-based resources encompass all types of health care, including primary care, laboratory testing, medical imaging, care provided to treat behavioral health conditions (e.g., care provided to treat mental health and substance use), and all types of specialty care (e.g., orthopedics). Community-based care may be constrained because care is completely unavailable, or is unavailable at certain times, for people with certain types of insurance, or for people who lack insurance. This may occur because a number of areas have provider shortages.[24] The federal government designates primary care health professional shortage areas and makes a number of programs available to alleviate these shortages. Still, there are approximately 6,100 areas designated as having too few primary care providers.[25] ED use may also be driven by the hours that physician offices are open, as EDs are often a source of after-hours care. For example, one study found that 75% of children's ED visits in 2012 occurred at night or on a weekend—hours when physicians offices are traditionally closed—and that this was the most common reason children visited an ED for non-emergent conditions, regardless of insurance status.[26]

EDs may be filling gaps in certain communities; but EDs may also be actively seeking patients, particularly those with private insurance coverage who are being treated for uncomplicated medical conditions.[27] As noted, ED care is more expensive for payors than is care provided in outpatient settings, in part, because hospitals receive higher reimbursements from payors to support the higher fix costs of an ED. Given these higher reimbursement rates, hospitals can generate revenue through the ED.[28] In these instances EDs may be filling gaps, but these gaps could have been filled in ways that are less expensive to payers.

EDs Provide Care to Safety Net Populations

ED use is also driven by the availability of community-based health service providers that accept safety net populations, such as the uninsured or Medicaid beneficiaries. For example, some physicians do not participate in Medicaid, and some Medicaid beneficiaries report barriers to accessing physician services.[29] This may also be true for uninsured individuals with few options except self-pay for visits, which may not be financially feasible.

Communities that have federal health centers—federally funded safety net facilities that are required to provide primary and some specialty and dental care to all individuals regardless of their ability to pay—have lower ED use.[30] Although health centers may employ strategies to reduce ED use,[31] they may be limited in their ability to do so because they are generally not open after hours and many may be operating at or above capacity.[32] Still, facilities that target the safety net population can reduce ED use, which demonstrates that some ED use is resource-sensitive.

EDs Provide Behavioral Health Care

EDs may fill gaps when needed behavioral health services are unavailable. Patients use EDs for behavioral health care because there may be few other options, because there are shortages of behavioral health providers. Specifically, there are approximately 4,000 areas designated as mental health professional shortage areas and more than half of U.S. counties do not have a practicing behavioral health provider.[33] In addition to provider shortages, there are also shortages of inpatient treatment options for patients who require longer-term treatment.[34] This occurs, in part, because a number of states have decreased funding for inpatient psychiatric care.[35] Patients with mental health conditions may also be brought to an ED by law enforcement when the person is causing a disturbance that law enforcement or other emergency personnel determine requires medical intervention. Although such episodes may be acute, they may not necessarily be best addressed in an ED. Some EDs may lack the services or staff necessary to provide behavioral health care and even in cases when EDs do not lack capacity, providing care to this population is resource intensive. This is particularly the case for patients with both behavioral health conditions and acute or chronic health conditions.[36] A study conducted by the Agency for Healthcare Research and Quality (AHRQ) and the Substance Abuse and Mental Health Services Administration (SAMHSA) found that individuals with mental health and/or substance use disorders that impaired their functioning were more likely to have multiple ED visits during the course of a year (to treat both physical and behavioral health conditions).[37] This was particularly true for individuals who had co-occurring chronic conditions such as diabetes.

EDs May Not Be Used Appropriately

In part because of the ED's role as a gap filler, conventional wisdom holds that some ED visits are inappropriate when patients use EDs for minor ailments or for convenience.[38] Although some EDs visits are inappropriate (i.e., these visits are to treat conditions that could have been treated in an outpatient setting),[39] researchers have found that this generally occurs because people have few other treatment options or because they were referred to an ED by a health care provider.[40] This is particular true for Medicaid enrollees, where public (and policy maker) perceptions are that Medicaid enrollees misuse EDs.[41] However, the data do not suggest this because EDs more often evaluated Medicaid enrollees as having an urgent or semi-urgent complaint than were privately insured patients seen in the ED.[42] Although Medicaid enrollees use EDs at higher rates than people who are privately insured or uninsured, much of this use can be explained by the higher rates of chronic conditions among Medicaid enrollees, or by Medicaid enrollees' difficulties in securing an appointment with another provider.[43] Because they lack access to other providers, uninsured individuals may use EDs for health conditions that could have been treated in an outpatient setting (e.g., diabetes), but were not because of access issues.

Some of the contention that patients use EDs unnecessarily may be an artifact of the terminology that EDs use to classify visits. EDs use the Emergency Severity Index (ESI) to triage patients, which uses the term "non-urgent" to indicate that wait times should not exceed 24 hours.[44] "Non-urgent" complaints do not equate to "unnecessary" complaints. The ESI system categorizes complaints based on needed resources, physical assessment, and risk factors and may classify visits as "non-urgent" based on the severity of the complaint. However, it is often difficult to determine prospectively whether a complaint is non-urgent. Patients may present to EDs with a complaint that they perceive as a true emergency, for instance, receiving an uncomplicated bite from a feral animal. Most people, even educated clinicians, recognize this condition as requiring prompt care; however, because the bite is uncomplicated, it is categorized as "non-urgent." This coding system makes it difficult to determine whether EDs are being used inappropriately because some cases classified as non-urgent may have seemed urgent when the patient presented to the ED.

EDs Provide Primary Care

In addition to filling gaps in available primary care, EDs are also taking on some of the role that primary care providers (PCPs) once filled by evaluating and managing chronic illnesses, particularly for older adults.[45] Patients with chronic illnesses may require rapid evaluation and possible treatment; therefore, PCPs and other providers are increasingly referring these patients to EDs.[46] Medical advances have expanded the scope of illnesses treatable in the ED setting because EDs generally offer a number of diagnostic tests that are not readily or simultaneously available in other settings.[47] This expanded diagnostic role of EDs occurs in part for clinical reasons, but it is also driven by administrative factors such as a patient's ability to secure a timely visit with a physician that is included in the patient's insurance plan.[48] The decision to admit a patient to a hospital after rapid diagnostic testing is increasingly being made by an ED physician, which offsets a 24% decline in admissions from PCPs.[49]

Though EDs have resources to evaluate patients with chronic illnesses, PCPs are better equipped to manage these patients in the long-term. In general, EDs are not designed to manage chronic illness, and ED provision of this type of care may be detrimental to patients. ED providers do not generally have the patient's full medical records—although increased use of electronic health records could change this—and given the nature of an ED environment, providers face frequent interruptions and are often rushed because of incoming emergencies. This may mean that patients who seek primary care in an ED can receive lower-quality care and are at greater risk of experiencing a medical error than if the care was received in a more appropriate setting.[50] Such unintended consequences, may, in turn, create a feedback loop where these patients require additional ED care.

EDs Are a Gateway for Inpatient Admissions

Generally, EDs are considered to be costly for a hospital because they have high fixed costs related to their emergency capacities, which may not be used on a daily basis. However, depending on a hospital's payor mix, EDs may generate revenue for a hospital because they drive inpatient admissions.[51] Specifically, between 2003 and 2009, the total number of hospital admissions increased driven primarily by a 20% increase in non-elective admissions from EDs.[52] Even in cases where an ED visit does not result in an admission, ED visits for individuals who are privately insured can be profitable.[53] This is particularly true when EDs are treating uncomplicated conditions that could have been treated in an outpatient setting.[54] However, ED visits may not be profitable with other payers; outpatient visits for those enrolled in Medicare or Medicaid or who are uninsured may yield reimbursement rates that are lower than the hospital's costs. Despite the potential of such losses, EDs can be profitable overall because of their link to admission; as a consequence, some hospitals have expanded ED services or have created freestanding emergency rooms. Some hospitals are also anticipating that EDs will become revenue generating with the ACA's expansion of private insurance coverage.[55] Although EDs may be profitable for a hospital, particularly when EDs are used to treat uncomplicated conditions, such ED care is generally costly to payors because care could be provided at a lower cost in an outpatient setting.[56]

With 15% of ED visits resulting in admissions,[57] these admissions compose nearly half of all hospital admissions and over two-thirds of all non-elective admissions.[58] ED visits that result in admission are particularly common for Medicare beneficiaries. In 2010, sixty percent of ED visits by Medicare beneficiaries resulted in a hospital admission.[59] Although ED visits represent a large percentage of all acute care visits, they account for 2% of all Medicare costs.[60] This outcome occurs partially because when Medicare beneficiaries are admitted after an ED visit, the payment for ED services is included within Medicare's payment for inpatient services.[61] As ED visits for Medicare beneficiaries are more likely to result in an admission,[62] total ED costs are generally underestimated.[63]

The ACA May Affect ED Use

The implementation of the Affordable Care Act (ACA) may have a number of effects on the use of EDs and their finances, although these effects vary by hospital and depend on the patients they treat. The ACA is generally expected to increase hospital reimbursements for emergency care because fewer people will be uninsured and therefore seeking uncompensated care in an ED.[64] However, insurance coverage rates are expected to vary, in part, because some states will not implement the ACA Medicaid expansion.[65] In states that have implemented the ACA Medicaid expansion, the effects of the ACA are more pronounced because a larger share of the population has gained insurance coverage. Specifically, hospitals in these states report that their expenditures on uncompensated care have decreased since the ACA was implemented.[66] In states that did not implement the ACA Medicaid expansion, these declines have not occurred, but these hospitals are still subject to a number of ACA-related payment reductions that were enacted, in part, because it was expected that the law would decrease the amount of uncompensated care that hospitals would provide. Hospitals that see payment reductions, without concurrent increases in collections, may be further strained by the ACA.[67]

The effects of the ACA on ED use are not yet clear. It is possible that the law may decrease ED use, may slow the rate of ED growth, or keep the growth of ED use comparable to the growth that would have occurred without changes.[68] Or it may decrease ED use for certain groups, as one study of ED use by young adults found.[69] However, it is possible that the law may increase ED use; researchers have found that ED use is higher among the newly insured and that ED use increased for those who became Medicaid-eligible in Oregon, a state that had previously implemented a Medicaid expansion.[70] Such increases in ED use could be temporary, as people with unmet needs seek care once they gain coverage, but then use drops as their health care needs are met.[71] ACA could also mean that ED patients are sicker than the ones ED treated prior to the law; as was found in a study of ED use in Massachusetts, a state that enacted health reforms prior to the ACA.[72] Although the full effects of the ACA on ED use are not yet known, use will likely vary by state, and may change over time. In addition, there are concerns that some people newly eligible for Medicaid may not be able to secure timely access to primary care or specialty care providers, and may continue to seek care in the ED.[73]

New Types of Health Care Facilities May Change the EDs' Role

Three new outpatient health care options may change the role of the ED by filling gaps in outpatient and after-hours care. Retail clinics provide unscheduled routine primary care; and may provide some access to care for non-emergency conditions for individuals who are able to pay for such services. Similarly, urgent care clinics provide unscheduled and after-hours access to care for a larger range of services. Hospitals may also choose to operate free-standing emergency rooms that function like an ED, but are not located on hospital grounds. These facilities, if operated by a hospital, would be subject to EMTALA. Other entities—such as private investment groups or ED physicians—have also opened free-standing emergency rooms, which are not subject to EMTALA[74] (see *Text Box 3*). Although these options have the potential to enhance ED function by lessening the EDs' role as a gap filler, it is also possible that their growth may adversely affect EDs, because these facilities tend to be located in areas where patients have high rates of private insurance and these facilities are not required to accept all patients, and therefore, may limit their patients to those with private insurance, a potential source of revenue to EDs. As such, these new provide types could draw insured patients from traditional EDs, making the remaining patients disproportionately uninsured or on Medicaid, which could strain EDs' finances.[75]

Text Box 3: Retail Clinics, Urgent Care Clinics, and Free Standing EDs

Retail Clinics provide quick care for routine medical complaints (e.g., bronchitis). They generally lack access to laboratories, x-rays, or diagnostic equipment. They are located in a retail location, such as a pharmacy, and may be affiliated with a hospital or health system. They are most often staffed by a nurse practitioner or a physician assistant and generally require the patient (or the patient's insurance) to pay the cost of services and often require payment at the time that services are rendered.

Urgent Care Clinics are generally free-standing physicians' offices that offer extended hours and on-site access to laboratory testing, x-rays, and other diagnostic equipment. They offer more services than are available at a retail clinic (e.g., they can treat fractures). They generally require the patient (or the patient's insurance) to pay the cost of services and often require payment at the time that services are rendered.

Free-Standing Emergency Rooms provide services similar to the care available in an ED, but without the co-located hospital available for admission or certain surgeries. These facilities, unless operated by a hospital, are generally not subject to EMTALA, and are not required to accept Medicare and Medicaid reimbursements. As such, they may disproportionately serve patients with private insurance. Many free-standing EDs have transfer agreements with hospitals and some are operated by the hospitals they refer patients to (thereby increasing admissions for patients with private insurance at the referral hospital).

Sources: Ateev Mehrotra et al., "Retail Clinics, Primary Care Physicians, and Emergency Departments: A Comparison of Patients' Visits," Health Affairs, vol. 27, no. 5 (September 2008), pp. 1272-1282; Robin M. Weinick, Rachel

M. Burns, and Ateev Mehrotra, "Many Emergency Department Visits Could Be Managed at Retail Clinics or Urgent Care Centers," Health Affairs, vol. 29, no. 9 (September 2010), pp. 1630-1636; American College of Emergency Physicians, Members of the Emergency Medicine Practice Committee, Freestanding Emergency Department: An Information Paper, American College of Emergency Physicians, July 2013, https://www.acep.org /uploadedFiles/ACEP/Practice_Resources/issues_by_category /administration/Freestanding%20Emergency%20Departments%200713.pdf and Beth Kutscher, "New Points of Entry: Stand-alone ERs Offer Systems Path to Higher Volume," Modern Healthcare, October 5, 2013.

FEDERAL REGULATION AND SUPPORT OF ED SERVICES

The federal government both regulates and supports ED services by (1) requiring hospitals with EDs to provide certain emergency services, (2) reimbursing for emergency services provided to individuals enrolled in federal insurance programs, (3) requiring certain private insurance plans to include coverage of emergency health services, and (4) providing funds to hospitals to defray the cost of providing uncompensated care. The federal government also supports hospital preparedness as part of its emergency preparedness activities, and supports the broader health care delivery system in ways that might reduce inappropriate ED use. Specifically, it supports health care safety net facilities, behavioral health care, and efforts to increase care coordination to reduce ED use for individuals with chronic conditions. Examples of federal involvement in hospital-based emergency care are discussed below.[76]

Emergency Medical Treatment and Active Labor Act (EMTALA)

The federal government requires—as a condition of Medicare participation—that hospitals with dedicated EDs screen and provide treatment to patients with emergent conditions regardless of a patient's ability to pay.[77] This requirement is set forth in the Emergency Medical Treatment and Active Labor Act (EMTALA), which was enacted in 1986 as part of the Consolidated Omnibus Budget Reconciliation Act of 1985 (P.L. 99-272). EMTALA was enacted in response to controversies that arose when patients died because some hospitals refused emergency services to uninsured patients as a way of reducing the amount of uncompensated care the hospitals provided. This practice is known as "dumping."[78] EMTALA requires that patients be medically evaluated—through an appropriate medical screening exam (MSE)—and that patients be transferred to a hospital that can provide necessary services if the screening hospital is unable to provide appropriate care.

Hospitals have discretion about the types of specialty physicians they have available on-call.[79] If a hospital lacks an appropriate on-call physician to treat a particular patient it may transfer the patient to a facility that has an appropriate physician available.[80] A number of hospitals have difficulty in recruiting specialists to provide ED on-call coverage. For a number of reasons, specialty physicians may not want to take ED call. One reason is liability risk (or perceptions of that risk). Individual physicians are not subject to EMTALA; instead, hospitals are and may be sued by private individuals who are injured as a result of a hospital not meeting its EMTALA requirements.[81] Physicians cannot be sued for injuries incurred as a result of an EMTALA violation, but may be liable for injuries to ED patients that result from errors or negligence on the part of the treating physician.[82] Physicians may perceive this liability to be high and may feel at a greater risk when treating ED patients because they often treat these patients quickly, without complete knowledge of their underlying medical conditions. Specialty physicians may also not wish to take ED call because, if they do, they are required—under the hospital's EMTALA requirement—to respond within a designated time frame[83] or face a fine ($50,000) and possible exclusion from the Medicare program.[84] The lack of specialty physicians willing to take ED call may have a larger impact on health care access. Some hospitals are unable to secure specialty physicians—a particular issue for high-risk specialties (e.g., neurosurgery)—and have to close their ED[85] or divert patients to other hospitals with these specialists. This may create a feedback loop whereby patients do not seek care at these hospitals because the hospital does not offer the full range of services, which may make it difficult for the hospital to remain open.[86]

Although EMTALA permits hospitals to bill patients who receive care as a result of the requirement, EMTALA has created the perception to some patients that EDs are a source of free care for the uninsured and that EDs must provide full treatment to patients even if they present with non-emergent conditions. These perceptions, in turn, may drive ED use for the uninsured, as ED use is often used for non-acute, non-emergent conditions by uninsured individuals.[87] In addition, though hospitals bill uninsured patients, the amounts that hospitals receive from uninsured patients are generally less than those received from insured patients. In some cases, the uninsured may be billed at higher rates than those billed to insurers; however, not all uninsured individuals will pay for services because some are unable to do so, and because some hospitals have indigent-care programs that provide free or reduced care.[88]

Tax-Exempt Hospitals and Charity Care

Not all hospitals have EDs, although some states require hospitals to have an ED to be licensed.[89] In states without this requirement, the entity that operates the hospital determines whether or not a hospital has an ED. Specifically, hospitals that are not-for-profit or those operated by state and local governments are more likely to have an ED—nearly all these types of hospitals have an ED, whereas only two-thirds of investor-owned hospitals do.[90] Not-for-profit and state and local hospitals operate EDs and provide charity care (i.e., uncompensated care) as part of their missions.[91] In addition, the ACA requires that hospitals that have tax-exempt status meet a "community benefit standard," although this can be satisfied in a number of ways; some hospitals do so by providing free or reduced care.[92]

Coverage of Emergency Care and Federal Insurance Programs

The federal government finances care provided to beneficiaries enrolled in Medicare, Medicaid, and CHIP. Under each of these programs, emergency services are a covered benefit. As such, beneficiaries are eligible to receive services in EDs with hospitals receiving reimbursements that vary by the services provided, the program providing reimbursements, and the location and type of hospital providing services.[93] Emergency health services are also considered to be an "essential health benefit" under the ACA. As such, non-grandfathered private insurance plans offered through the nongroup and small group markets must cover emergency services.[94] Together, Medicare, Medicaid, CHIP, and private insurance plans offered through ACA exchanges provide insurance coverage to approximately 120 million people or approximately 37% of the U.S. population.[95]

Federal Support for Uncompensated Care

The costs associated with hospitals providing uncompensated care have been defrayed by three federal sources: Medicare disproportionate share hospital (DSH) payments, Medicaid DSH payments, and payments for undocumented immigrants. Through the Medicare and Medicaid programs, the federal government provides DSH payments to hospitals that treat large numbers of low-income patients. Although these payments can be used to support uncompensated care provided by an ED, in some cases they are not. Instead, in some states DSH payments are used to defray uncompensated inpatient care costs or all of the uncompensated care that a hospital provides.[96] The ACA, because it was expected to reduce the size of the uninsured population, included changes to Medicare and Medicaid DSH payments. Subsequent laws have amended Medicaid DSH payment reductions and delayed these reductions until FY2017.[97]

Hospitals also receive reimbursements for some emergency care provided to unauthorized aliens, nonimmigrants and legal permanent residents who are not eligible for Medicaid because, for the latter, there is a five-year waiting period before legal permanent residents are eligible for Medicaid.[98] These reimbursements are for services that qualify as "Emergency Medicaid," and cover services from emergency providers (including hospitals, but also including emergency transport) that treat an emergency or services for a pregnant woman that are related to her pregnancy (including prenatal care, labor, delivery, and post-partum care).[99] "Emergency Medicaid" is not available for all of the conditions for which people seek treatment in an ED, nor are these funds available for services provided to all unauthorized aliens, nonimmigrants, or legal permanent residents; "Emergency Medicaid" funds are only available for services provided to individuals who would have otherwise qualified for Medicaid, which, unless a state has implemented the Medicaid expansion, does not include childless adults.[100]

In addition to reimbursements available from Medicaid, from FY2005 to FY2008, the federal government allotted annual funding to states for certain emergency care provided to undocumented aliens.[101] The federal funding was allotted to the six states with the highest number of undocumented alien apprehensions receiving one-third of total funding. States, in turn, provide or have provided funding to hospitals, physicians, and ambulance service providers for emergency services provided to eligible patients. Although funding has not been allotted since FY2008, some states still have funds remaining from their allocation. As of May 2014, twenty-nine states have exhausted their allocation under this program, so new claims for services are not being accepted in these states. Although this funding source is or was available, for some hospitals it may not represent full reimbursement for care provided. This occurs in part because it is difficult to determine a particular hospital's need for these funds because hospitals do not ask about a patient's immigration status when providing care.

Emergency Preparedness

The federal government supports hospital emergency preparedness through the Hospital Preparedness Program administered by the HHS Assistant Secretary for Preparedness and Response (ASPR). The program began in FY2002, and funding for the program peaked in FY2003 with an appropriation of $515 million; funding since that time has declined by nearly 50% as the program's FY2014 appropriation was $255 million.[102] The program awards grants to support the ability of communities and hospitals to provide surge capacity during a public health emergency. Although these grants do not support day-to-day ED operations, support to strengthen medical surge capacity may include the development of processes to enhance ED operations so that hospitals have the capacity to surge during an emergency.[103]

Trauma Care

ASPR also has authority to award grants to support trauma care, although these grants have not been funded.[104] Trauma care is a specific type of care, provided in designated centers that provide more intensive services than those that are traditionally available in an ED.[105] Trauma centers are distinct from EDs, but generally trauma centers will also have an ED. In the absence of a designated trauma center, EDs provide care to severely injured patients until they can be transferred to an appropriate trauma center. Given issues of ED crowding, funding to support designated trauma centers may mean that EDs would provide less trauma care prior to a transfer, which could free up ED resources.

Healthcare Safety Net

The federal government supports general health infrastructure, including the health care safety net. This support is not specifically related to emergency care, but has the potential to reduce ED use by reducing the ED's need to fill health system gaps. Determining whether or not this occurs is difficult as these programs do not directly aim to reduce ED use. For example, HHS's Health Resources and Services Administration (HRSA) supports the development of the health care workforce, focusing particularly on providers who care for disadvantaged populations. Such support does not focus on reducing ED use, but may reduce the need for some resource-sensitive ED use.[106] In an effort more focused on reducing ED use, HRSA awards grants to support federal health centers that provide primary care, dental care, and behavioral health care to all individuals regardless of their ability to pay.[107] Research has found that these health centers reduce ED use, in particular, for conditions that could have been treated in an outpatient setting (e.g., asthma).[108]

The Centers for Medicare & Medicaid Services (CMS), the agency that administers the Medicare, Medicaid, and CHIP programs, has awarded funds to states as part of its $50 million Emergency Room Diversion Grant Program. The program seeks to increase the number of community health centers, extend the hours at existing centers, and better coordinate care as part of CMS's efforts to reduce ED use among Medicaid beneficiaries. Grants were awarded to 20 states from FY2006 through FY2009.[109]

Behavioral Health Support

EDs provide behavioral health care services because these services are often unavailable in the community. County-level data suggest that counties with available behavioral health outpatient options have lower ED use for behavioral health conditions.[110] The federal government, through SAMSHA, supports efforts to increase access to behavioral health care; though such support is not specifically related to emergency care, SAMHSA programs might reduce ED use.

Specifically, SAMHSA support includes formula and competitive grants to states and territories to support community-based mental health and substance abuse treatment and prevention services.[111] Competitive grants to support these services are available to other entities, including private organizations and local communities. SAMHSA also provides technical assistance and workforce support. Given that provider shortages limit access to behavioral health care such support could help ensure that behavioral health services are available.[112]

CMS has also awarded funds to states to test whether reimbursing certain psychiatric facilities to which Medicaid payments have traditionally been prohibited would reduce Medicaid costs for psychiatric patients.[113] These prohibited facilities are called Institutions for Mental Disease (IMDs); they are inpatient facilities that have more than 16 beds and a patient roster in which more than half of the patients have severe mental illness. Traditionally, Medicaid has not been able to reimburse these facilities for services they provide to Medicaid beneficiaries between the ages of 22 and 64.[114] Some experts believe that the exclusion increases ED use.[115] This CMS-funded demonstration will examine health care costs overall, but given high ED use for behavioral health care conditions, this demonstration could provide information about whether reimbursing these facilities lowers ED use.

Care Coordination

The federal government also supports care coordination through medical homes, accountable care organizations, and other mechanisms.[116] Care coordination generally aims to improve health and reduce costs by preventing the exacerbations of chronic conditions that may necessitate an ED visit. A number of ongoing federal initiatives are administered by CMS, and as such, these initiatives focus on coordinating care as a way of reducing costs for beneficiaries of these programs. As discussed further below, a number of these initiatives include efforts to reduce ED use.

Research

The federal government supports medical research primarily through the National Institutes of Health (NIH).[117] Within the NIH, it supports the NIH's Office of Emergency Care Research (OECR).[118] This office aims to coordinate emergency care related research across the various NIH institutes and centers. A number of institutes within the NIH support emergency care research, generally in the context of a given disease or population that the institute focuses on (e.g., the National Heart, Lung, and Blood Institute supports research on cardiac emergency care and/or the National Institute on Aging supports research on emergency care for older adults).[119] OECR serves a broader coordination function and attempts to identify funding opportunities related to emergency care and/or those related to treating emergent medical conditions. It does not directly fund research grants. This NIH office is relatively new; it began in 2012 as a result of NIH efforts that followed up on the IOM emergency care reports.[120]

Selected Issues Affecting EDs

Nationwide, EDs have developed different strategies to deliver the care most appropriate to their respective communities. Despite differences, EDs generally face three common challenges to their ability to effectively provide care: (1) they are crowded, (2) they must provide repeat care to frequent users who could be more effectively treated in other settings, and (3) they must provide (or attempt to provide) care to patients with behavioral health conditions. Not all EDs will face these challenges because many of these concerns are related to the population that the ED serves. Hospitals that serve patients who have greater access to health care because they are privately insured or have Medicare coverage may not experience these challenges. Some hospitals have also developed strategies that have alleviated these concerns, or have implemented some of the strategies noted below. Still a number of EDs face these three challenges, which are defined and discussed below.

Crowding

Crowding is a situation in which the need for services exceeds an ED's capacity to provide these services. It often entails patients experiencing long wait times and/or being treated or monitored in non-treatment areas (e.g., hallways).[121] Generally, crowding reflects dysfunctions in the health care system; although it seems like an ED problem, it is actually a systemic problem.[122] As discussed, EDs fill gaps in the health care system. In some communities, or for some populations, EDs may be the only available health care option.[123] This gap-filling role, coupled with fewer available EDs, has resulted in crowded conditions at the remaining available EDs.[124] Research shows that crowding reduces access to timely care by causing EDs to divert ambulances and by contributing to long wait times, in some cases so long that patients choose to leave without being seen (LWBS).[125] Diverted ambulances and patients who LWBS typically travel to the next closest ED; this may cause another ED to become crowded, in turn, causing a domino effect among the area's remaining EDs. Crowding also reduces a hospital's capacity to absorb surges in patient volume, both daily and in the event of a public health emergency.[126]

Crowding occurs disproportionately in hospitals in urban areas, (referred to as metropolitan statistical areas [MSAs]), which make up two-thirds of all hospitals and provide 85% of all ED care.[127] Crowding is particularly common in MSAs where the growth in the health care infrastructure has not kept pace with population growth. Hospitals in MSAs are more crowded; as a result, they divert more ambulances and have longer wait times.[128] MSA hospitals generally treat patients in their adjacent areas, and may also receive patients from further away because they offer specialty services (e.g., trauma or burn care). Under EMTALA, hospitals offering such specialty services must accept transferred patients requiring this care; hospitals have to accept these patients even if their EDs are already crowded, which may further increase crowding.[129]

Causes of Crowding

Crowding results from a number of health system factors; specifically, it is a symptom of the mismatch in the larger supply and demand of health care services.[130] ED crowding is often examined through the "input-throughput-output model," which helps identify factors from the perspective of an ED[131] (see *Figure 1*). Although the model presents a number of factors that cause crowding; boarding—where hospitals keep admitted patients in an ED until a bed is available—is generally considered to be the primary cause of crowding.[132] Hospitals may board admitted patients because they lack inpatient beds or because they lack nursing staff to care for additional admitted patients.[133] In some cases, hospitals may have inpatient beds available, but these beds may be reserved for patients with particular conditions (because nurses and other staff are trained to care for patients with particular ailments) or may be reserved for elective surgical procedures, resulting in a situation where a person is boarded in an ED even though the hospital has a physical bed available.[134] Admitted patients may be boarded in an ED for hours or days. Generally, patients who are boarded have worse outcomes, including higher death rates and longer lengths of stay.[135] Boarded patients, by virtue of requiring an inpatient admission, are often the sickest patients in an ED; as such, their presence further exacerbates crowding because they consume ED resources that would otherwise be available for incoming emergencies. Although boarding is the primary cause of crowding, a number of health system changes could alleviate crowding, as the “input-throughput-output model” indicates.[136]

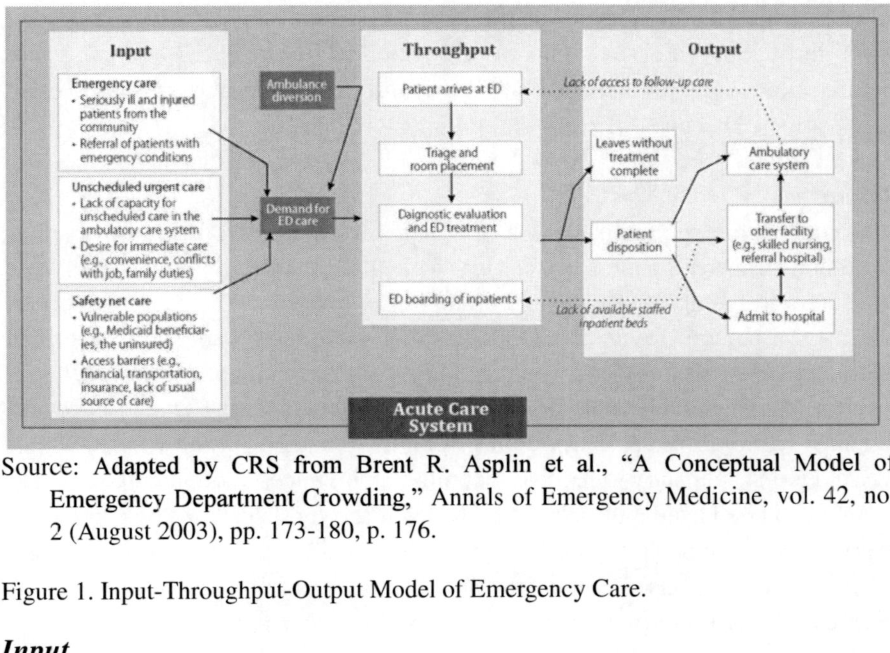

Source: Adapted by CRS from Brent R. Asplin et al., “A Conceptual Model of Emergency Department Crowding,” Annals of Emergency Medicine, vol. 42, no. 2 (August 2003), pp. 173-180, p. 176.

Figure 1. Input-Throughput-Output Model of Emergency Care.

Input

Input is any condition, event, or system characteristic that contributes to the demand for emergency care, unscheduled urgent care, or safety net care.[137] The demand for ED care depends on the volume of patients requiring emergency care and the volume of patients who are seeking care in the ED because it is after-hours or because they lack another source of care (e.g., safety net patients).[138] When the ambulatory care system is unable to provide the community with these kinds of services, people turn to the ED, thereby increasing demand.

Throughput

Throughput factors are events that influence a patient’s length of stay (LOS) in an ED. A person’s LOS is the length of time from arrival to discharge and involves two phases: (1) triage and room placement, and (2) diagnostic testing, ED treatment, and discharge.[139] Throughput factors, for example, are the number of CT scans, laboratory tests, and medications a person will need; whether the ED physician will have to consult a specialist; or how long it takes to see a physician initially. The model includes boarding in the throughput phase because it occurs within the ED and affects department operations; however, boarding results from a shortage of inpatient beds and should be considered separately from throughput factors that are under the control of the ED. The health of the population that the ED serves may also affect throughput. For example, as the population ages, ED patients may require more care to manage chronic conditions, including specialty care, which some EDs have difficulty obtaining.[140]

Output

Output refers to the disposition of a patient from an ED, including hospital admission, transfer to another facility, patient discharge, or patient death. It also refers to the ability of the ambulatory care system to provide appropriate care after a person leaves an ED. A hospital's available capacity determines whether an ED can transfer admitted ED patients to the inpatient unit. When a hospital lacks available beds or inpatient nursing staff, the ED will keep the patient (i.e., board the patient), either in hallway beds or in the rooms, which may reduce the capacity to receive incoming ambulances and patients.

Inpatient bed availability varies by hospital and by specialty. Some hospitals reserve medical inpatient beds for elective surgical procedures, even when its ED is holding patients.[141] Hospitals have a number of financial incentives to reserve beds for these procedures, including the higher reimbursement rate for certain elective procedures and the guarantee of being paid for elective procedures because insurance coverage is checked before procedures are scheduled.[142] As such, some hospitals have incentives to make sure that beds are filled and attempt to schedule surgeries to do so, meaning that few beds will be unoccupied and available for ED patients.[143]

Shortages of beds in particular specialties may disproportionally affect crowding and the outcomes of ED patients. Shortages of beds in psychiatric units may be a particular contributor to crowding, as behavioral health patients are boarded on average twice as long as those waiting for hospital beds.[144] Given that behavioral health patients are generally resource intensive, their boarding may disproportionately contribute to crowding.[145] Shortages of intensive care unit (ICU) beds are a particular concern for ED patients who require such care. These patients are particularly vulnerable, the number of these patients has increased, and they have higher mortality rates when they are not promptly moved to the ICU setting.[146]

The Effects of Crowding

Crowding affects the health care delivery system at multiple levels. Specifically, it affects patients, hospitals, and payers. It does so primarily through increased costs and adverse health outcomes because treatment is delayed or forgone.

Effects on Patients

Crowding reduces access to critical ED care by delaying the time in which patients are able to receive treatment, which may affect patient health. Specifically, for some conditions treatment must occur during a critical period or there will be adverse outcomes. Some of the symptoms of crowding, such as LWBS, ambulance diversion, and boarding also have specific effects on patients' health. For example, patients who LWBS would not be evaluated for a medical emergency that could have been prevented. Crowding may cause an ED to initiate ambulance diversion, which affects both the patient and the community. Ambulance diversion[147] extends the patient's length of time in the ambulance, the length of time to see a physician, and the length of time before the ambulance can respond to other emergencies.[148] Boarding can have particular health effects on elderly patients, who generally have worse outcomes when compared to patients with similar characteristics who were not boarded.[149] Finally, when patients are admitted to a unit or a physician's service, it is expected that they will receive a specific combination of treatments; however, an ED may not have the appropriate equipment or staff who know how to perform these specific combinations of treatments. Inpatient units have specialized staff, strict nurse-to-patient ratios, and daily routines—all of which aim to provide the appropriate standard of care to meet a patient's needs.

Effects on Hospitals

Crowding, in general, and boarding, in particular, affects hospital finances by reducing ED and inpatient volume and decreasing revenue earned from serving additional patients. Each time an ambulance is diverted or patient LWBS, hospitals lose an opportunity to bill. One study on a single hospital calculated that reducing wait times by 120 minutes or less could increase revenue nearly $4 million dollars over the course of a year. It also found that moving boarded patients to inpatient beds within two hours increased the annual "functional treatment capacity" of an ED by 10,397 hours, or 433 days.[150] Boarding also increases length of stay; for example, one study found that patients who board for over 24 hours experienced a 12% longer hospital stay.[151] When hospitals are paid under a fixed-payment scheme (such as are used by Medicare),[152] it is in the hospital's financial interest to reduce the length of stay so that the patient's costs do not exceed the predetermined payment amount, as the hospital must absorb the additional costs.

Hospitals may also wish to reduce crowding and ED wait times to attract patients. Some hospitals—particularly those trying to attract private insured patients—will publicly advertise wait times as part of their marketing.[153] In addition, CMS publicly reports certain hospital-level quality data, including measures related to ED wait times and some that are affected by ED crowding, (e.g., measures related to pain management and timely antibiotic administration).[154] Prospective patients can use these data to select a hospital that has better ED outcomes and shorter wait times.[155] Some of these ED measures are also linked to Medicare payment under the Hospital Inpatient Quality Reporting Program; as such, hospitals face financial penalties based on their reporting of some of the ED-related measures.[156]

Crowding may also be costly to hospitals because it can contribute to hospital-level nursing shortages. EDs often have more difficulty filling staff vacancies due to the intensity of emergency care.[157] Crowding can exacerbate this issue because it could increase staff turnover among ED nurses, leaving the hospital with more vacancies to fill. It may also leave hospitals with a more junior nursing staff because more experienced staff may be more likely to leave.[158] Researchers have found that increased patient-care demands push experienced staff to leave their jobs, in part, because of decreased job satisfaction, but also because some staff may fear that conditions are jeopardizing patient safety and are putting them at risk of losing their licenses (physicians may also have liability concerns because of these increased patient care demands).[159] Such concerns would also apply to ED physicians and may make it difficult for some hospitals to recruit and retain their services.[160] The effect of crowding on staffing and staff turnover also adds to a hospital's financial pressures, because it is costly to recruit staff and new staff requires training— for example, new ED nurses require months of training to obtain the basic skills needed to deliver ED care.[161]

Effects on Payers

Crowding may increase health care costs for payers. It may also have particular costs for the Medicare program, because it is the largest payer for inpatient care.[162] As crowding can delay treatment, it increases the likelihood that patients will experience adverse events—an injury that results from medical intervention and not the patient's underlying medical condition—

which are more common in older adults.[163] Adverse events are costly to payers because they often require additional medical treatment beyond the original medical condition that caused the patient to seek care in the ED.[164]

Strategies That May Reduce Crowding

A number of strategies may reduce crowding; generally, such strategies focus on ways that hospitals can reduce boarding by increasing the number of inpatient beds available.[165] For example, hospitals may consider the following strategies:

- Moving boarders to inpatient halls: doing so places boarded patients in a quieter, less crowded, and a better-staffed setting that has been shown to be safe. It also frees up emergency department beds and can expedite the patient being placed in a proper inpatient bed.
- Undertaking active bed management, by appointing a single person to track beds (e.g., a "bed czar"), by using a computer system to track beds, or other methods to address system-level bottlenecks.
- Using "reverse triage," which employs a system designed for creating capacity during disasters by discharging patients who have a low need for an inpatient bed.
- Smoothing elective surgical schedules by distributing procedures evenly over the week to decrease peaks in demand for inpatient beds and the need to cancel procedures because beds are not available.
- Implementing the "four hour rule": this rule, implemented in the United Kingdom and Western Australia, requires EDs to evaluate, treat, discharge, or admit patients in four hours or less.[166] Although this policy reduces boarding, some have raised concerns that it may reduce the quality of care because it encourages EDs and hospitals to discharge patients early, when it may not be medically appropriate.[167]

A number of current programs may also reduce boarding. For example, in 2012, CMS required hospitals to report data related to boarding and ED length of stay. The public reporting of these data and their inclusion in some CMS quality programs may provide hospitals with incentives to reduce crowding. The Medicare program requires that hospitals meet certain conditions to participate in the Medicare program (called conditions of participation).[168] One of these conditions is that hospitals must be accredited, although hospitals can choose to be accredited by a state regulatory organization, often hospitals will seek to be accredited by the Joint Commission,[169] which accredits and certifies health care organizations. The Joint Commission adopted requirements—effective January 1, 2014—that hospitals address boarding for the purposes of accreditation.[170] Both CMS's and the Joint Commission's changes are new, so the full effects are not yet known, but both policy changes may incentivize hospitals to reduce crowding.[171]

Frequent ED Users

Another issue affecting ED care is that of frequent ED users. Although no formal definition exists, for purposes of this report, a frequent user is an individual who uses an ED multiple times a year.[172] Frequent users represent a small number of ED users overall, but account for a high number of total ED visits. One study, for example, estimated that frequent users (defined in the study as individuals with three or more visits annually) represented 29% of all ED users but 60.4% of all ED visits.[173] Although most frequent ED users have high rates of chronic conditions, anecdotal evidence and media reports have fueled a misconception that frequent ED users are a disadvantaged population who unnecessarily use EDs for conditions that could be treated in an ambulatory setting.[174] Frequent users are a concern for policy makers because (1) they contribute to crowding; (2) they increase costs for payers, including government payers; and (3) their ED use may reflect poor care coordination in other settings (e.g., they lack primary care or coordinated primary and specialty care to manage their asthma and seek care at an ED for an asthma attack).Frequent users are not a monolithic group; as such, policy options need to target the different types of frequent users.[175] Frequent ED users can be divided into three broad sub-categories, based on utilization patterns: frequent non-emergent users (i.e., people who use EDs frequently to treat conditions that do not require emergency care), high-cost health system users, and very frequent ED users. The causes of ED visits differ by the three types as do the policy levers that could be employed to reduce the number of frequent visits (see *Table 2*).

Table 2. Three Types of Frequent ED Users

Type	Characteristics of Frequent ED Users	Consequences and Solutions
Frequent Non-emergent Users	• have barriers to primary care • most have private insurance and a regular PCP	• costly to payers because care provided in an ED is more expensive than care provided in an ambulatory

Type	Characteristics of Frequent ED Users	Consequences and Solutions
	• lack access to afterhours care • have lower rates of chronic illness than other frequent ED users	setting • health system changes to improve access can reduce the number of these users and the number of visits per user
High-Cost Health System Users	• tend to "shop" for providers • visit EDs between four and nine time per year • have substantial burdens of chronic illness (which increases as the number of visits increase) • consider themselves to be in fair-to-poor health or are severely disabled • are more likely to be between the ages of 25 and 44, or older than 64 • have high rates of underlying substance use or mental illness; however, treatment for these conditions represents a small share of visits • most visits are for injuries, hypertension, heart conditions, pneumonia or bronchitis, and mental disorders • are likely to arrive in an ambulance	• most expensive of the three types of frequent ED users because they are more likely to require more expensive inpatient care • policies that encourage care coordination can reduce this type of use • policies that target these users may also need to include social and economic issues that may present barriers to accessing health care
Very Frequent ED Users	• have 10 or more visits per year • are less likely to have a regular PCP • visit multiple EDs • make up a very small portion of all ED users • more likely to be male • have high rates of disability and/or have multiple chronic illnesses • visit often for substance use or mental illness • have complex medical, mental, economic factors contributing to ED use, such as homelessness or serious mental illness. • high rates of current or previous substance abuse, mental illness, or both	• users are costly, but are less likely to be admitted than the high-cost health system users • policies that encourage care coordination can reduce this type of use, but these patients have low provider loyalty, which needs to be accounted for when designing programs • policies that target these users may also need to include social and economic issues that may present barriers to accessing health care

Sources: John Billings and Tod Mijanovich, "Improving the Management of Care for High-Cost Medicaid Patients." Health Affairs, vol. 26, no. 6 (2007), pp. 1643-1654; Malcolm Doupe et al., "Frequent Users of Emergency Departments: Developing Standard Definitions and Defining Prominent Risk Factors." Annals of Emergency Medicine, vol. 60, no.1 (2012), pp; 24-36; Eduardo LaCalle and Elaine Rabin, "Frequent Users of Emergency Departments: The Myths, the Data, and the Policy Implications." Annals of Emergency Medicine, vol. 56, no.1 (2010), pp 42-48; and Anna S. Sommers, Ellyn R. Boukus, and Emily Carrier, Dispelling Myths About Emergency Department Use: Majority of Medicaid Visits Are for Urgent or More Serious Symptoms, Center for Studying Health System Change, No. 23, Washington, DC, July 2012.

Strategies That Target Frequent Users

As *Table 2* demonstrates, changes to the ambulatory care system to make care more accessible and coordinated can reduce frequent ED use. Such strategies include adding additional providers, opening or expanding outpatient care settings (e.g., retail clinics; see "New Types of Health Care Facilities May Change the EDs' Role"), increasing provider hours, creating or expanding nurse advice lines, and expanding or initiating health education campaigns that encourage appropriate ED use.[176] Other strategies seek to prevent the need for ED use by managing chronic conditions, coordinating care across providers, and more frequently monitoring patients.[177] These strategies may also include analytic tools (e.g., electronic health records) to share data across providers.[178]

In attempts to control costs, CMS has initiated programs that focus on Medicare or Medicaid beneficiaries who are frequent health system users. CMS calls these "super-utilizer" programs. These programs do not necessarily focus on high-ED users, but may include *High-Cost Health System Users* and the *Very Frequent ED Users* because these users are expensive. Specifically, chronically ill individuals account for 5% of the total population but nearly half of all health care spending.[179] This pattern of concentrated spending also occurs among Medicaid beneficiaries, where 1% of the Medicaid population is responsible for 22% of the spending. Although not all of this spending occurs in EDs, EDs are a gateway for hospital admissions, where the bulk of this spending occurs. As such, managing chronic conditions so that ED visits are avoided may reduce costs. CMS is undertaking initiatives focused on super-utilizers, as are private payers and providers, such as hospitals. Though specific programs employed to target super-users vary, they generally involve methods to target the most appropriate program participants by trying to identify participants who exhibit characteristics that are consistent with having high-cost, preventable health care use.[180]

Payment Methods

A number of new payment models are being tested as a way to control costs; because they include incentives to coordinate care, they may also reduce frequent users.[181] Under a fee-for-service payment scheme, providers receive additional compensation for providing additional care, which may incentivize providing additional services to frequent users rather than coordinating care and seeking to prevent ED use for this group. Under alternate payment models that reward care coordination or provide incentives to achieve certain performance targets, providers lack such incentives. A number of the strategies undertaken to reduce super-users involve testing new payment methods (see *Text Box 4)*.

Text Box 4: Example Payment Models

- *Case Management Payment:* Fixed payment per-member-per-month to fund care coordination.
- *Multi-Payer Case Management Payment:* Payment for care coordination from the respective payer for each patient.
- *Per-Episode of Care Payment for Program Services:* Payment for each episode of care that is based on complexity of the patient.
- *Per-Member Per-Month:* A payment to a managed care organization that is used to fund both medical and behavioral health services that is adjusted to account for the patient's health status.
- *Shared Savings for Total Cost of Care*: A generally time-limited capitated payment to an agency to provide care to a group of patients. If the cost of providing care is less than the capitated payment, the agency gets a portion of the savings.

Source: Letter from Cindy Mann, Director Center for Medicaid and CHIP Services, "Targeting Medicaid Super-Utilizers to Decrease Costs and Improve Quality," July 24, 2013, http://medicaid.gov/Federal-Policy-Guidance/ Downloads/CIB-07-24-2013.pdf.

Federally Supported Care Coordination Models

The federal government has provided explicit support for the Medicare program and for state Medicaid programs to develop care coordination programs, that may, among other policy goals, reduce the number of super-utilizers by managing chronic conditions to reduce the number of times these patients seek ED care. Such federal support includes the following examples:

- *Accountable Care Organizations (ACOs)* are groups of health care providers that join together to provide coordinated care to a group of Medicare beneficiaries in exchange for a share of any savings realized from coordinating such care.[182] ACOs are eligible for shared savings if the Medicare spending for assigned beneficiaries falls below a historical benchmark and if they meet certain quality benchmarks.
- *Bundled Payment for Care Improvement Initiative (BPCI):* Selected health care organizations participate in a new payment model where the health care organizations are reimbursed for episodes of care. These payment arrangements aim to provide high-quality coordinated care.[183]
- *Medicaid Health Homes:* States may receive a higher Federal Medical Assistance Percentage (FMAP)—the percentage of the state's Medicaid program that the federal government pays[184]—to support interdisciplinary care provided by the health home team.[185]
- *Targeted Case Management:* States may add a Targeted Case Management (TCM) service to their Medicaid program to enhance existing health home or managed care models.[186]

Behavioral Health Care in EDs

EDs face two distinct behavioral health care challenges. The first is that EDs may be ill-equipped to treat patients who are primarily seeking care to treat a behavioral health condition. The second is that an increasing number of patients with physical health conditions also have behavioral health conditions, which makes treating their physical ailments more difficult.[187] In general, EDs are strained to provide the former and are challenged in providing the latter because these cases are resource-intensive and exacerbate already crowded conditions. The number of behavioral health- only visits has also increased rapidly, with the number of these visits growing at a rate four times higher than the growth in non-behavioral health visits.[188] Mental health and substance use disorders are generally not appropriate to treat in an ED because they are not acute conditions; instead, they require treatment and monitoring over time, which is not in concert with the type of services that EDs are designed to provide.[189] The major exception to this is an acute episode: either an acute psychiatric episode or an overdose or adverse drug reaction for individuals with substance use issues. These cases often present in an ED; they may be symptomatic of uncontrolled behavioral health conditions, but often an ED is the proper site of care in these instances.

Causes of Increased Behavioral Health Treatment in EDs

Generally, patients with behavioral health conditions present in an ED because of insufficient community resources available to manage the patients' needs. A number of communities have shortages of mental health and substance abuse services. Such shortages may also be underestimated because rates of both behavioral health conditions are underreported.[190] Community level conditions such as increases in drug use in certain communities (e.g., the recent increases in heroin use in certain communities) may also affect ED use for behavioral health conditions, as individuals who overdose or have adverse drug reactions may present to EDs.[191]

Insurance coverage may also contribute to behavioral health conditions being seen in EDs. An AHRQ/SAMSHA study found that uninsured individuals with behavioral health conditions were most likely to have had multiple ED visits during the course of a year. Among those seen in the ED, these individuals were least likely to be admitted.[192] This study also found that the likelihood of admission varied by patient characteristics (such as demographic characteristics), insurance status, and the size of the hospital (larger hospitals offered more specialty services and were more likely to admit patients). The use of an ED to provide behavioral health care, in particular for the uninsured population, may also contribute to the financial constraints that EDs face, as some of this care may be uncompensated.

Effects of Treating Behavioral Health Care in an ED

One of the major effects of treating behavioral health care in an ED is crowding. This occurs because EDs that lack behavioral health resources may board these patients while waiting to transfer them to an appropriate facility.[193] Such facilities are in short supply; therefore, some behavioral health patients may end up waiting in an ED for hours and often days for an available bed.[194] Patients with behavioral health conditions may also contribute to crowding because they may be more difficult to care for, thus requiring more staff resources than a patient without a behavioral health condition. Being treated in an ED may also be particularly stressful for individuals with certain mental health conditions because EDs by their very nature are chaotic. This might exacerbate certain mental health conditions. Treating these behavioral health patients in an ED may also be challenging because EDs lack many of the services that these patients need. For example, behavioral health patients often require consults from specialists (e.g., psychiatrists) who may not be on-site so patients must wait in the ED for such consults. Or EDs may not have needed detoxification services.

Treating behavioral health care in an ED could also contribute to crowding because emergency room procedures to triage patients with psychiatric conditions are less well-developed than those used to triage patients with physical ailments, which may complicate and delay treatment for patients.[195] Research has also found that ED providers do not feel comfortable providing care to emergency psychiatric patients, have received less training to do so, and believe that these patients may be more violent to ED staff.[196]

Strategies to Reduce ED Use for Behavioral Health Conditions

The availability of community behavioral health treatment can reduce the use of EDs for patients. For example, an AHRQ-SAMSHA study found that counties with community mental health centers had fewer ED visits for mental health conditions, as did counties with inpatient psychiatric and chemical dependency treatment facilities, which had fewer ED visits for people with behavioral health conditions.[197] Hospitals themselves can make inpatient psychiatric beds available or can create relationships with chemical dependency treatment facilities to which they can discharge ED patients with behavioral health conditions. Programs that seek to increase access to behavioral health care (see "Behavioral Health Support") can also reduce ED use.

Insurance coverage may also influence ED use for behavioral health services. For example, some treatment facilities do not accept Medicaid patients, so Medicaid patients often have fewer treatment options and may present to an ED. The implementation of the ACA, which requires behavioral health coverage by some private insurance plans,[198] coupled with federal parity requirements, should increase coverage for behavioral health conditions.[199] Increased coverage if coupled with access to community level providers could reduce ED use for behavioral health conditions because conditions would be better managed. It is unclear whether this would occur because federal parity requirements do not require all plans to include behavioral health coverage[200] and because provider shortages may prevent individuals who gain coverage to access behavioral health care services.[201]

POLICY LEVERS AVAILABLE TO CONGRESS

To alleviate some of the issues raised regarding emergency care, Congress might consider using various policy levers, including (1) oversight, (2) reimbursement changes to federal programs, (3) directed spending, (4) changes to statutory mandates, and (5) watchful waiting. Congress may also consider a combination of these levers. The discussion below is not exhaustive, but it represents options that Congress may consider to address some of the emergency care concerns raised in this report.

Oversight

Congress has oversight of executive branch agencies, which it may leverage to improve ED operations. For example, it could conduct oversight hearings on topics related to ED care, or it could investigate the efforts of involved federal agencies to improve ED care. Congress has used its oversight in this area in the past; for example, it has commissioned GAO reports in this area.[202] Congress may consider holding a hearing (or a series of hearings) on topics related to ED care. Congress may also consider requesting a report or reports in this area, to be undertaken by the involved federal agencies (e.g., CMS, SAMSHA), GAO, or another entity. Such oversight might motivate HHS to address some of the considerations discussed in this report, even in the absence of other congressional activity.

Changes to Federal Program Requirements

As mentioned, hospitals must meet certain conditions, including being accredited by the Joint Commission or another entity,[203] to participate in the Medicare program (called conditions of participation).[204] Medicare can influence hospital processes by amending its conditions of participation and requiring the Joint Commission to accredit hospitals based on this amended criteria. For example, as part of its accrediting process, the Joint Commission requires that hospitals develop procedures for boarding, including the boarding of psychiatric patients.[205] To improve ED function, the Medicare program could encourage (or require) the Joint Commission to amend its accreditation criteria to encourage or require hospital-level changes that would affect ED flow, such as placing a cap on the number of elective admissions a hospital can have when the ED is boarding patients, or requiring that hospitals smooth their elective surgery schedule so that surgeries are scheduled throughout the week instead of clustered on certain days.[206]

Medicare could also consider amending its conditions of participation to improve ED functioning in emergencies. This strategy is currently under consideration as CMS proposed, in December of 2013, to strengthen emergency preparedness requirements for all Medicare and Medicaid participating hospitals. The new conditions of participation would require hospitals to have emergency preparedness programs and emergency preparedness plans.[207]

Directed Spending

Congress may consider providing funding to support programs or payments that may alleviate ED delivery issues. Congress could do so either through entitlement programs, such as Medicare and Medicaid, or through discretionary programs. In some cases, statutory changes may be required to create new programs or to extend funding in cases where authorized funding has expired.

Spending and Reimbursement Through Mandatory Programs

A number of the challenges that EDs face are financial. As such, the federal government may consider whether hospitals require additional funding to support ED services or whether current funding sources (e.g., Medicare and Medicaid reimbursements) are sufficient. For example, some hospitals provide uncompensated care to individuals who are not eligible for Medicaid because of their immigration status. Though funds had been appropriated to defray the cost of this care, they have not been appropriated since FY2010; however, hospitals may be able to discharge some of their ED spending for those ineligible for Medicaid because of their immigration status through "Emergency Medicaid."[208] Congress could consider whether "Emergency Medicaid" is sufficient or could consider appropriating targeted funds to support hospitals that provide high volume of uncompensated care to undocumented immigrants, similar to the program that existed until FY2010. Congress could also consider the current system of DSH payments and whether such payments are sufficient and/or whether these payments are adequately targeted so that the hospitals with the highest burdens of uncompensated care receive these payments. Congress could consider whether a different funding source that provides explicit funding for emergency care under EMTALA is warranted, as an expert group that reviewed EMTALA requirements recommended.[209] As discussed, efforts to prevent ED use may lower costs; as such, Congress may wish to consider whether past efforts—such as the Emergency Room Diversion Grant program[210]—that aim to reduce ED use by increasing the services available to Medicaid beneficiaries were successful at reducing ED use and whether such efforts should be continued and/or expanded. Congress may also wish to examine whether current efforts that seek to reduce ED use by coordinating care and preventing exacerbations of chronic conditions are sufficient and if such efforts should be expanded.

Congress may also consider changes to reimbursement policies in federal programs that affect ED functioning. For example, Emergency Medical Services (EMS) brings patients to an ED who could have been stabilized elsewhere because, in some cases, EMS systems are not reimbursed unless the patient is brought to a hospital. This reimbursement policy may create incentives to transport patients to an ED in instances when it may not be medically necessary to do so.[211] Experts suggest that changes to reimbursement policy could mean that fewer patients are transported to EDs, thereby reducing ED crowding and lowering costs in general.[212]

Some have suggested that Medicaid psychiatric hospitals reimbursement policies constrain the supply of available psychiatric beds and that those reimbursement policies should be amended.[213] Medicaid prohibits payment to Institutions for Mental Disease (IMDs) for services rendered to adults between the ages of 22 and 64.[214] IMDs are inpatient facilities with more than 16 beds and a patient roster in which more than half of the patients have severe mental illness. Some suggest that this exclusion makes it difficult to obtain care for individuals in this age range with Medicaid coverage.[215] The Medicaid IMD exclusion may contribute to ED crowding in two ways: (1) it constrains treatment options, leading individuals to seek care in an ED, and (2) once an individual seeks care in the ED, it constrains discharge options, which may lead to boarding.

Spending Through Discretionary Programs

Hospitals face a number of challenges related to providing primary and behavioral health care in part because of provider shortages. The federal government makes investments in supporting primary care both at the facility and at the provider level. Options could be considered to target these investments in areas where EDs are particularly crowded or where ED use for primary care is particularly common. Similar strategies could be employed for targeting federal behavioral health investments. Some recent evidence suggests that urgent care centers that focus on treating the mentally ill have reduced ED use in certain areas;[216] policy makers could evaluate whether such centers could be expanded and whether federal investments are needed to do so.

ED use is also particularly common among the homeless population, which often lacks other sources of care or may have untreated behavioral health care needs. Although the federal government supports health centers for the homeless,[217] some homeless individuals may seek care in EDs or may be brought to EDs by law enforcement during a psychiatric episode. Research on frequent users has found that homelessness is an underlying cause of frequent ED use.[218] Congress may consider, as a way of reducing ED use (and associated costs), providing additional resources to support health care for the homeless or by providing resources to better coordinate health and social services.

In addition to specific funding to hospitals for services provided, Congress could consider providing support for emergency care research or the emergency care workforce. Currently the NIH has the Office of Emergency Care Research (OECR)[219] to coordinate emergency care research. This office does not have dedicated funding to support general research on emergency care. Instead, NIH/OECR coordinates research on emergency care needed to treat specific diseases or populations. As such, there is little support for research that focuses on emergency care as a system; such research may be useful to develop policies or procedures that could alleviate ED delivery system concerns. Congress may also wish to consider whether the current emergency care workforce is sufficient; and if Congress determines that it is not, it may wish to consider providing support to develop and sustain the emergency care workforce.[220]

Congress may also consider appropriating funds to support the development of crowding quality measures. At present, a number of measures are used to quantify crowding, such as the Emergency Department Work Index, or ED occupancy rate;[221] CMS also collects data on similar measures such as LWBS, and “time spent in the ED before being sent home,”[222] but these measures do not reflect the full scope of crowding because they do not reflect the full input/throughput/output model of crowding.

Changes to Statutory Mandates

EMTALA is the major federal statutory mandate that governs ED care.[223] As such, Congress may consider a number of statutory changes to EMTALA that could improve the flow of ED patients. Specifically, it could consider implementing a number of recommendations made by the EMTALA Technical Advisory Group (TAG) to the HHS Secretary in 2007.[224] The TAG made the following recommendations, which could address some of the issues raised in this report:[225]

- Require hospitals with specialized behavioral health capabilities, to accept the transfer of patients who are gravely disabled or a danger to themselves or others, or who have an emergent medical condition, if the receiving hospital has the resources and capacity to provide appropriate care.
- Amend the EMTALA statute to include liability protection for hospitals, physicians, and other licensed independent practitioners who provide services to patients as part of the hospital's EMTALA requirement. Others have suggested providing broader liability protections that are not exclusive to providers serving under the hospital's EMTALA requirements, but that would apply to EMTALA care (see *Text Box 5*).
- Require that hospitals and medical staff develop and revise an annual plan for on-call coverage that includes, at a minimum, evaluation of the following factors: (1) advertised and licensed hospital capabilities and services provided, (2) community demand for ED services as determined by ED visits, (3) transfers out of hospital for emergency services, (4) physician resources, and (5) past call plan performance.

Text Box 5: Standard of Care

Some policy makers have considered specifying standards of care that health care providers must provide (e.g., providers must adhere to standard clinical guidelines) and would require that medical liability claims be reviewed to determine whether the health care provider followed these guidelines. Such standards/guidelines are intended to reduce the number of medical liability claims.

Although such standards would apply to health care providers broadly, they may lessen the liability concerns of ED physicians (and on-call specialists).

Sources: See, for example, in the 113th Congress, H.R. 4106, H.R. 4757, and S. 1769 and Table A-1in CRS Report R41661, Medical Malpractice Liability Reform: Legal Issues and 50-State Surveys on Tort Reform Proposals.

In addition to the TAG's recommendation, Congress may also consider amending the EMTALA statute or the regulations that implement EMTALA to specify that if an ED does not have the capacity to take on additional patients, but the hospital has available inpatient capacity, the inpatient unit must board the patients who would have otherwise been boarded in the ED.[226]

Watchful Waiting

Watchful waiting is an option that is always available to Congress. If, for example, Congress determines that many of the challenges that EDs face are driven by the uninsured population or by fragmented care in the delivery system, Congress may consider waiting to see whether the implementation of the ACA's insurance expansion or the ACA's care coordination initiatives alleviate some or all of the current challenges. For this or a number of other reasons, Congress may allow the situation to unfold without further congressional involvement.

Concluding Observations

Improving how EDs function will require system-wide changes in health care delivery, as ED care is affected by a number of factors in the health care delivery system beyond an ED's control. Doing so may have the corollary benefit of reducing health care costs, because ED care is more costly than providing similar treatment in an outpatient setting. In addition, the current delivery challenges that EDs face increase costs because they delay patients' access to timely services. A number of health system factors affect ED care, including insurance coverage; the availability of inpatient hospital care; and the availability of outpatient providers, in general, after hours, and their willingness to accept particular insurance types. Several of these health system factors are in flux, and how such changes play out may improve or harm ED function. For example, the growth of urgent care, retail clinics, and efforts to expand access to insurance and better coordinate care may improve ED operations, but these changes may have unintended consequences and may not affect all EDs equally. Delivery system changes are also occurring in the midst of population-level changes, which may increase the need for ED services because the population is aging with higher rates of chronic disease. Taken together, the issue of ED use and its functioning may require monitoring because a number of the variables that affect it are evolving.

End Notes

[1] Marcus Ong Eng Hock et al., "Should Emergency Departments Be Society's Health Safety Net?" Journal of Public Health Policy, vol. 26, no. 3 (2005), pp. 269-281.

[2] CRS Report RS22738, EMTALA: Access to Emergency Medical Care. Note that hospitals bill patients and attempt to recover the cost of treatment, and hospitals are not required to provide care to patients who present to EDs with conditions that do not require immediate treatment (i.e., non-emergent conditions).

[3] Agency for Health Care Research and Quality, "Overview of Emergency Department Visits in the United States, 2011," Statistical Brief #174, 2014.

[4] Acute care visits are those for short-term treatment for an injury, illness, or an urgent medical condition. By contrast, 20% of acute care visits were handled by a specialty physician, who account for 60% of the physician workforce. Stephen R. Pitts et al., "Where Americans Get Acute Care: Increasingly, It's Not at Their Doctor's Office." Health Affairs, vol. 29, no. 9 (September 2010), pp. 1620-1629.

[5] Ibid.

[6] Agency for Health Care Research and Quality, "Overview of Emergency Department Visits in the United States, 2011," Statistical Brief #174, 2014.

[7] Stephen R. Pitts et al., "Where Americans Get Acute Care: Increasingly, It's Not at Their Doctor's Office." Health Affairs, vol. 29, no. 9 (September 2010), pp. 1620-1629.

[8] Ibid. For information about access to care for Medicaid beneficiaries, see Department of Health and Human Services, Office of Inspector General, State Standards for Access to Care in Medicaid Managed Care, Washington, DC, September 2014, http://oig.hhs.gov/oei/reports/oei-02-11-00320.pdf.

[9] Studies have found that ED services can be three to five times more costly than similar services provided in a community-based setting. For discussion, see R.M. Coffey, Emergency Department Use for Mental Health and Substance Use Disorders, U.S. Agency for Healthcare Research and Quality (AHRQ), Rockville, MD, August 23, 2010, http://www.hcup-us.ahrq.gov/reports/ED_Multivar_Rpt_Revision_Final072010.pdf, p. 3.

[10] Institute of Medicine of the National Academies, Hospital-Based Emergency Care: At the Breaking Point (Washington, DC: National Academies Press, 2006); Institute of Medicine of the National Academies, Emergency Medical Services: At the Crossroads (Washington, DC: National Academies Press, 2006); and Institute of Medicine of the National

Academies, Hospital-Based Emergency Care for Children: Growing Pains (Washington, DC: National Academies Press, 2006).

[11] U.S. Government Accountability Office, Hospital Emergency Departments: Crowding Continues to Occur, and Some Patients Wait Longer than Recommended Time Frames, 09-347, April 2009, http://www.gao.gov/assets/290/ 289048.pdf; hereinafter, GAO-09-347.

[12] It is not yet clear whether the growth of retail clinics and urgent care centers will alleviate crowding and thereby enhance ED function. See "New Types of Health Care Facilities May Change the EDs' Role" in this report.

[13] The Patient Protection and Affordable Care Act (ACA, P.L. 111-148, as amended) expanded insurance coverage, which has reduced the number of people who are uninsured. For more information, see the CRS series of ACA Reports at http://www.crs.gov/ pages/ subissue.aspx?cliid=3746&parentid=13&preview=False. It is not clear what the effect of the ACA will be on ED use; see discussion in "The ACA May Affect ED Use" in this report.

[14] GAO-09-347.

[15] For example, one study found that expanding Medicaid coverage increased ED use among those who were newly Medicaid eligible. See Sarah L. Taubman et al., "Medicaid Increases Emergency-Department Use: Evidence from Oregon's Health Insurance Experiment," Science, vol. 343, no. 6 (January 17, 2014), pp. 263-268.

[16] Centers for Medicare & Medicaid Services, Office of the Actuary, National Health Statistics Group, Year 2012. For descriptions of Medicare and Medicaid, see CRS Report R40425, Medicare Primer.

[17] Though ED spending is a relatively small percentage of overall Medicare spending (approximately 2%). Medicare beneficiaries are increasingly admitted to hospitals through EDs and 25% of Medicare spending is for inpatient hospital services. Jeffrey M. Gonzalez, National health Care Expenses in the U.S. Civilian Noninstitutionalized Population, 2011, Agency for Healthcare Research and Quality, Medical Expenditure Panel Survey, Statistical Brief #425, Rockville, MD, November 2013, http://meps.ahrq.gov/mepsweb/ data_files/publications/st425/stat425.pdf and Medicare Payment Advisory Commission (MedPAC), National Health Care and Medicare Spending, Washington, DC, June 2014, http://www.medpac.gov/documents/publications/june-2014-data-book-section-1-national-health-care-andmedicare-spending.pdf?sfvrsn=2.

[18] CRS Report RL31719, An Overview of the U.S. Public Health System in the Context of Emergency Preparedness.

[19] See, for example, the federal health center program described in CRS Report R42433, Federal Health Centers, and programs that the federal government administers through the Health Resources and Services Administration, described in CRS Report R43304, Public Health Service Agencies: Overview and Funding.

[20] This report focuses on emergency departments (EDs) that are available to the general population; as such, it does not include EDs that are operated by the Departments of Defense or Veterans Affairs or those operated by the Indian Health Service.

[21] Trauma care is provided at trauma centers, which are specialized hospitals with the staffing, resources, and equipment needed to treat severely injured patients. They provide specialized care beyond that of an ED. Not all hospitals with EDs are trauma centers, but most trauma centers have EDs. See Centers for Disease Control and Prevention, "Access to Trauma Care: Getting the Right Care, at the Right Place, at the Right Time," August 24, 2010, http://www.cdc.gov/traumacare/access_trauma.html.

[22] Institute of Medicine of the National Academies, Hospital-Based Emergency Care: At the Breaking Point (Washington, DC: National Academies Press, 2006).

[23] Agency for Health Care Research and Quality, "Overview of Emergency Department Visits in the United States, 2011," Statistical Brief #174, 2014.

[24] CRS Report R42029, Physician Supply and the Affordable Care Act.

[25] U.S. Department of Health and Human Services, Health Resources and Services Administration, "Shortage Designation: Health Professional Shortage Areas & Medically Underserved Areas/Populations," http://www.hrsa.gov/ shortage/index.html. Approximately 4,000 areas have been designated as having shortages of mental health providers.

[26] Renee M. Gindi and Lindsey I. Jones, Reasons for Emergency Room Use Among U.S. Children: National Health Interview Survey, 2012, U.S. Department of Health and Human Services, Centers for Disease Control and Prevention, National Center for Health Statistics, NCHS Data Brief: No. 160, Hyattsville, MD, July 2014.

[27] Michael Wilson and David Cutler, "Emergency Department Profits Are Likely to Continue as the Affordable Care Act Expands Coverage," Health Affairs, vol. 33, no. 5 (May 2014), pp. 792-799.

[28] Phillip L. Henneman et al., "Is Outpatient Emergency Department Care Profitable? Hourly Contribution Margins by Insurance for Patients Discharged from an Emergency Department," Annals of Emergency Medicine, vol. 63, no. 4 (April 2014), pp. 404-411.

[29] Peter J. Cunningham and Ann S. O'Malley, "Do Reimbursement Delays Discourage Medicaid Participation by Physicians?" Health Affairs, vol. 28, no. 1 (November 18, 2008), pp. w17–w28; Heidi Allen, Bill J. Wright, and Katherine Baicker, "New Medicaid Enrollees in Oregon Report Health Care Successes and Challenges," Health Affairs, vol. 33, no. 2 (February 2014), pp. 292-299; and Anna S. Sommers, Ellyn R. Boukus, and Emily Carrier, Dispelling Myths About Emergency Department Use: Majority of Medicaid Visits are for Urgent or More Serious Symptoms, Center for Studying Health System Change, No. 23, Washington, DC, July 2012.

[30] CRS Report R42433, Federal Health Centers.

[31] U.S. Government Accountability Office, Hospital Emergency Departments: Health Center Strategies that May Help Reduce Their Use, GAO-11-414R, April 11, 2011.

[32] Jessamy Taylor, Don't Bring Me Your Tired, Your Poor: The Crowded State of America's Emergency Departments, National Health Policy Forum, Issue Brief-No. 811, Washington, DC, July 7, 2006.

[33] U.S. Department of Health and Human Services, Health Resources and Services Administration, "Shortage Designation: Health Professional Shortage Areas & Medically Underserved Areas/Populations," http://www.hrsa.gov/ shortage/index.html and National Alliance on Mental Illness, NAMI State Advocacy: Workforce Development: Policy Brief, Arlington, VA, June 2011, http://www.nami.org/Content/NavigationMenu/State_ Advoca cy/About_the_Issue/ Workforce_Development_2011.pdf.

[34] CRS Report R43255, The Mental Health Workforce: A Primer, and Centers for Medicare & Medicaid Services, Extract of Final Report of The Emergency Medical Treatment and Labor Act Technical Advisory Group to the Secretary of the U.S. Department of Health and Human Services, Washington, DC, April 2, 2008, https://www.cms.gov/Regulations-and-Guidance/Legislation/EMTALA/downloads/ EMTALA_Final_Report_Summary.pdf.

[35] Peter J. Cunningham, Kelly McKenzie, and Erin Fries Taylor, "The Struggle to Provide Community-Based Care to Low-Income People with Serious Mental Illness," Health Affairs, vol. 25, no.3 (2006), pp. 694-705. It is possible that as some states implement the ACA's Medicaid expansion, mental health services may become more accessible.

[36] Anne Manton, Care of the Psychiatric Patient in the Emergency Department, Emergency Nurses Association, white paper, Des Plaines, IL, February 2013, http://www.ena.org/practice-research/research/Documents/ WhitePaperCareofPsych.pdf.

[37] R.M. Coffey, Emergency Department Use for Mental Health and Substance Use Disorders, U.S. Agency for Healthcare Research and Quality (AHRQ), Rockville, MD, August 23, 2010, http://www.hcup-us.ahrq.gov/reports/ ED_Multivar_Rpt_Revision_Final072010.pdf.

[38] Anna S. Sommers, Ellyn R. Boukus, and Emily Carrier, Dispelling Myths About Emergency Department Use: Majority of Medicaid Visits are for Urgent or More Serious Symptoms, Center for Studying Health System Change, No. 23, Washington, DC, July 2012.

[39] Kristy Gonzalez Morganti et al., The Evolving Roles of Emergency Departments in the United States, RAND Health, RR-280-ACEP, Santa Monica, CA, 2013, http://www.rand.org/pubs/research_reports/RR280.html; hereinafter, RANDHealth ED Report.

[40] Ibid.

[41] As a result of this perception and in an attempt to reduce non-emergency ED use, some state Medicaid programs have instituted copayments for non-emergency ED use. See Medicaid and CHIP Payment Advisory Commission, MAC Facts, Key Findings on Medicaid and CHIP: Revisiting Emergency Department Use in Medicaid, Washington, DC, July 2014.

[42] Urgent refers to conditions assessed to need an evaluation within one hour and semi-urgent refers to conditions needing an evaluation between one and two hours. See Anna S. Sommers, Ellyn R. Boukus, and Emily Carrier, Dispelling Myths About Emergency Department Use: Majority of Medicaid Visits are for Urgent or More Serious Symptoms, Center for Studying Health System Change, No. 23, Washington, DC, July 2012.

[43] Medicaid and CHIP Payment Advisory Commission, MAC Facts, Key Findings on Medicaid and CHIP: Revisiting Emergency Department Use in Medicaid, Washington, DC, July 2014.

[44] GAO-09-347.

[45] Stephen Pitts et al., "National Trends in Emergency Department Occupancy, 2001 to 2008: Effect of Inpatient Admissions Versus Emergency Department Practice Intensity," Annals of Emergency Medicine, vol. 60, no. 6 (December 2012). Some experts have also speculated that the use of EDs to manage chronic illness will increase as the population ages. Institute of Medicine of the National Academies, Hospital-Based Emergency Care: At the Breaking Point (Washington, DC: National Academies Press, 2006).

[46] RANDHealth ED Report.

[47] Ibid.

[48] Ibid. Hospitals have some control over these administrative factors (e.g., they contract with certain physicians who, in turn, only contract with certain insurance plans) and some hospitals promote ED referrals as a way of increasing inpatient admissions. See discussion in "EDs Are a Gateway for Inpatient Admissions."

[49] Ibid; and Derek DeLia and Joel Cantor, Emergency Department Utilization and Capacity, Robert Wood Johnson Foundation, 2009.

[50] There is evidence that medical errors in EDs are linked to interruptions, which are more common in an ED setting. See Carey D. Chisholm et al., "A Task Analysis of Emergency Activities in Academic and Community Settings," Annals of Emergency Medicine, vol. 58, no. 2 (January 31, 2011), pp. 117-122.

[51] Michael Wilson and David Cutler, "Emergency Department Profits Are Likely to Continue as the Affordable Care Act Expands Coverage," Health Affairs, vol. 33, no. 5 (May 2014), pp. 792-799.

[52] Hospital admissions are comprised of two types: non-elective admissions and elective admissions. Non-elective admissions refer to medically necessary admissions to treat unscheduled events, such as a heart attack. Elective admissions are generally procedures that are medically necessary; however, they are planned (e.g., a knee replacement).

[53] Michael Wilson and David Cutler, "Emergency Department Profits Are Likely to Continue as the Affordable Care Act Expands Coverage," Health Affairs, vol. 33, no. 5 (May 2014), pp. 792-799.

[54] Phillip L. Henneman et al., "Is Outpatient Emergency Department Care Profitable? Hourly Contribution Margins by Insurance for Patients Discharged from an Emergency Department," Annals of Emergency Medicine, vol. 63, no. 4 (April 2014), pp. 404-411.

[55] Michael Wilson and David Cutler, "Emergency Department Profits Are Likely to Continue as the Affordable Care Act Expands Coverage," Health Affairs, vol. 33, no. 5 (May 2014), pp. 792-799.

[56] Studies have found that ED services can be three to five times more costly than similar services provided in a community-based setting. For discussion, see R.M. Coffey, Emergency Department Use for Mental Health and Substance Use Disorders, U.S. Agency for Healthcare Research and Quality (AHRQ), Rockville, MD, August 23, 2010, http://www.hcup-us.ahrq.gov/reports/ED_Multivar_Rpt_Revision_Final072010.pdf, p. 3.

[57] Derek DeLia and Joel Cantor, Emergency Department Utilization and Capacity, Robert Wood Johnson Foundation, 2009.

[58] RANDHealth ED Report.

[59] Centers for Disease Control and Prevention, Ambulatory Health Care Data: National Ambulatory Medicare Care Survey, National Hospital Ambulatory Medicare Care Survey: 2010 Emergency Department Summary Tables, Hyattsville, MD, February 24, 2014, pp. 6-7, http://www.cdc.gov/nchs/data/ahcd/nhamcs_emergency/ 2010_ed_web_tables.pdf.

[60] ED visits account for 2% of costs for Medicare beneficiaries and account for 4% of total Medicaid spending; see Jeffrey M. Gonzalez, National Health Care Expenses in the U.S. Civilian Noninstitutionalized Population, 2011, Agency for Healthcare Research and Quality, Medical Expenditure Panel Survey, Statistical Brief #425, Rockville, MD, November 2013, http://meps.ahrq.gov/mepsweb/data_files/publications/st425/stat425.pdf and Medicaid and CHIP Payment Advisory Commission, MAC Facts, Key Findings on Medicaid and CHIP: Revisiting Emergency Department Use in Medicaid, Washington, DC, July 2014.

[61] Medicare Payment Advisory Commission (MedPAC), Hospital Acute Inpatient Services Payment Basics, Payment Basics, Washington, DC, October 2013, http://www.medpac.gov/documents/payment-basics/hospital-acute-inpatientservices-payment-system.pdf?sfvrsn=0. This is also true for other payers where the hospital's charges for emergency care are included in the admission fee. ED physicians will bill patients separately. See Phillip L. Henneman et al., "Is Outpatient Emergency Department Care Profitable? Hourly Contribution Margins by Insurance for Patients Discharged from an Emergency Department," Annals of Emergency Medicine, vol. 63, no. 4 (April 2014), pp. 404-411.

[62] Centers for Disease Control and Prevention, Ambulatory Health Care Data: National Ambulatory Medicare Care Survey, National Hospital Ambulatory Medicare Care Survey: 2010 Emergency Department Summary Tables, Hyattsville, MD, February 24, 2014, pp. 6-7, http://www.cdc.gov/nchs/data/ahcd/nhamcs_emergency/ 2010_ed_web_tables.pdf.

[63] Other payers, including Medicaid, also include ED services as part of the reimbursement for a patient's inpatient services.

[64] Jessica E. Galarraga and Jesse M. Pines, "Anticipated Changes in Reimbursements for U.S. Outpatient Emergency Department Encounters After Health Reform," Annals of Emergency Medicine, vol. 63, no. 4 (April 2014), pp. 412- 417.

[65] For information about states having the option to implement the Medicaid expansion, see CRS Report R43564, The ACA Medicaid Expansion.

[66] Thomas DeLeire, Karen Joynt, and Ruth McDonald, Impact of Insurance Expansion on Hospital Uncompensated Care Costs in 2014, U.S. Department of Health and Human Services, Office of the Assistant Secretary for Planning and Evaluation, ASPE Issue Brief, Washington, DC, September 24, 2014, http://aspe.hhs.gov/health/reports/2014/ UncompensatedCare/ib_UncompensatedCare.pdf.

[67] For information on the ACA-related payment reductions, see "Federal Support for Uncompensated Care." Much of the information available about how hospitals will fare in Medicaid expansion and non-expansion states is anecdotal; for example, see Beth Kutscher, "Two Americas: Hospitals See Big Differences Between Medicaid Expansion and Nonexpansion States," Modern Healthcare, August 18, 2014, pp. 20-21.

[68] Soumy Karlamangla and Doug Smith, "Since Obamacare, Rate of Growth in L.A. County ER Visits Slows," LA Times, August 21, 2014, p. 2 and Christopher Chen, Gabriel Scheffler, and Amitabh Chandra, "Massachusetts' Health Care Reform and Emergency Department Utilization," The New England Journal of Medicine, vol. 365, no. e25 (September 22, 2011), pp. 1-3.

[69] Tina Hernandez-Boussard, "Emergency Department Use: The Affordable Care Act Reduces Emergency Department Use by Young Adults: Evidence from Three States," Health Affairs, vol. 33 (September 2014), pp. 1648-1654.

[70] Mark McClelland et al., "The Affordable Care Act and Emergency Care," American Journal of Public Health, vol. 104, no. 10 (October 2014), pp. e8-e10 and Sarah L. Taubman et al., "Medicaid Increases Emergency-Department Use: Evidence from Oregon's Health Insurance Experiment," Science, vol. 343, no. 6 (January 17, 2014), pp. 263-268. Research on Massachusetts, another state that expanded its Medicaid program prior to the ACA, did not find increases in ED use for the Medicaid population. See Medicaid and CHIP Payment Advisory Commission, MAC Facts, Key Findings on Medicaid and CHIP: Revisiting Emergency Department Use in Medicaid, Washington, DC, July 2014.

[71] Nigel Lo et al., Increased Service Use Following Medicaid Expansion is Mostly Temporary: Evidence from California's Low Income Health Program, UCLA Center for Health Policy Research, Policy Brief, Los Angeles, CA, October 15, 2014, http://healthpolicy.ucla.edu/ publications/search/pages/detail.aspx?PubID=1338.

[72] Christopher Chen, Gabriel Scheffler, and Amitabh Chandra, "Massachusetts' Health Care Reform and Emergency Department Utilization," The New England Journal of Medicine, vol. 365, no. e25 (September 22, 2011), pp. 1-3.

[73] For information about access to care for Medicaid beneficiaries, see Department of Health and Human Services, Office of Inspector General, State Standards for Access to Care in Medicaid Managed Care, Washington, DC, September 2014, http://oig.hhs.gov/ oei/reports/oei-02-11-00320.pdf.

[74] Beth Kutscher, "New Points of Entry: Stand-alone ERs Offer Systems Path to Higher Volume," Modern Healthcare, October 5, 2013 and American College of Emergency Physicians, Members of the Emergency Medicine Practice Committee, Freestanding Emergency Department: An Information Paper, American College of Emergency Physicians, July 2013, https://www.acep.org/uploadedFiles/ACEP/Practice_ Resources/

issues_by_category/administration/Freestanding%20Emergency%20Departments% 200713. pdf.

[75] See, for example, Robin M. Weinick, Rachel M. Burns, and Ateev Mehrotra, "Many Emergency Department Visits Could Be Managed at Urgent Care Centers and Retail Clinics," Health Affairs, vol. 29, no. 9 (September 2010), pp. 1630-1633; and Alexa Ura, "Texas Hospitals Say They've Lost Insured Patients to Urgent Care," The New York Times, August 29, 2014, p. A19A, National Edition.

[76] The federal government also supports emergency medical services through the Department of Transportation; however, this support focuses on emergencies outside the hospital, which is beyond the scope of this report. For more information on these programs, see "Emergency Medical Services: National Highway and Transportation Safety Administration, (NHTSA)," at http://www.ems.gov/educationstandards.htm.

[77] Hospital-based EDs are required to provide care per EMTALA; however, the act only refers to stabilizing procedures and not to all services available within an ED or within a hospital in general. Some hospitals provide necessary treatment as dictated and transfer patients to other facilities for a variety of reasons: insurance, specialty needs, patient request, or bed availability.

[78] Mark M. Moy, The EMTALA Answer Book: 2009 Edition (Wolters Kluwer Law & Business, 2009), p. xxxiv.

[79] Letter from Director, Survey and Certification Group, Center for Medicaid and Medicare Services to Associate Regional Administrators, Division of Medicaid and State Operations, Region I-X, June 13, 2002, On-Call Requirements - EMTALA.

[80] Ibid.

[81] CRS Report RS22738, EMTALA: Access to Emergency Medical Care.

[82] Ibid.

[83] 42 C.F.R. §489.20(r)(2) does not define a specific time, instead it requires that a hospital define available providers.

[84] CRS Report RS22738, EMTALA: Access to Emergency Medical Care.

[85] Renee Y. Hsia, Arthur L. Kellermann, and Yu-Chen Shen, "Factors Associated with Closures of Emergency Departments in the United States," Journal of the American Medical Association, vol. 305, no. 19 (May 18, 2011), pp. 1978-1985.

[86] Centers for Medicare & Medicaid Services, Extract of Final Report of the Emergency Medical Treatment and Labor Act Technical Advisory Group to the Secretary of the U.S. Department of Health and Human Services, Washington, DC, April 2, 2008, https://www.cms.gov/Regulations-and-Guidance/Legislation/EMTALA/downloads/ EMTALA_Final_Report_Summary.pdf.

[87] Renee M. Gindi and Lindsey I. Jones, Reasons for Emergency Room Use Among U.S. Children: National Health Interview Survey, 2012, U.S. Department of Health and Human Services, Centers for Disease Control and Prevention, National Center for Health Statistics, NCHS Data Brief: No. 160, Hyattsville, MD, July 2014.

[88] Glenn A. Melnick and Katya Fonkych, "Hospital Pricing and the Uninsured: Do the Uninsured Pay Higher Prices?" Health Affairs, vol. 27, no. 2 (March 2008), pp. w116-w122.

[89] See for example, New York Code, Public Health, Article 28, §2801, "Definitions," at http://codes.lp.findlaw.com/ nycode/PBH/28/2801.

[90] Jessamy Taylor, Don't Bring Me Your Tired, Your Poor: The Crowded State of America's Emergency Departments, National Health Policy Forum, Issue Brief-No. 811, Washington, DC, July 7, 2006.

[91] Ibid.

[92] CRS Report RL34605, 501(c)(3) Hospitals and the Community Benefit Standard.

[93] For descriptions of Medicare, Medicaid, and CHIP, see CRS Report R40425, Medicare Primer; CRS Report R43357, Medicaid: An Overview; and CRS Report R43627, State Children's Health Insurance Program: An Overview.

[94] CRS Report R42069, Private Health Insurance Market Reforms in the Affordable Care Act (ACA). For discussion of grandfathered plans, see CRS Report R41166, Grandfathered Health Plans Under the Patient Protection and Affordable Care Act (ACA).

[95] CRS analysis of data from Department of Health and Human Services, Center for Medicare & Medicaid Services, Medicaid & CHIP: February 2014 Monthly Applications, Eligibility Determinations, and Enrollment Report, Baltimore, MD, April 4, 2014; U.S. Department of Health and Human Services, "Medicaid Enrollment Grows by More than 3 Million," press release, April 4, 2014, http://www.hhs.gov/healthcare/facts/blog/2014/04/medicaid-chip-determinations-february.html; and Kaiser Family Foundation at http://kff.org/medicare/state-indicator/total-medicarebeneficiaries/; and U.S. Census Bureau.

[96] Lavonne Downey et al., "Who Pays? How Reimbursement Impacts the Emergency Department," Journal of Health and Human Services Administration, vol. 36, no. 4 (Spring 2014), pp. 400-416.

[97] For more information on Medicaid DSH payments, see CRS Report R42865, Medicaid Disproportionate Share Hospital Payments. For information on ACA changes to Medicare DSH payments, see CRS Report R41196, Medicare Provisions in the Patient Protection and Affordable Care Act (PPACA): Summary and Timeline.

[98] CRS Report R43561, Treatment of Noncitizens Under the Affordable Care Act.

[99] 42 C.F.R. §440.255 "Limited services available to certain aliens." CRS Report R40772, Noncitizen Health Insurance Coverage and Use of Select Safety-Net Providers.

[100] The expansion of Medicaid in the ACA permitted states to cover childless adults, but not all states have elected to expand their Medicaid programs. See CRS Report R43564, The ACA Medicaid Expansion.

[101] Unless otherwise noted, this paragraph is drawn from Department of Health and Human Services, Centers for Medicare & Medicaid Services, Section 1011: Federal Reimbursement of Emergency Health Services Furnished to Undocumented Aliens, ICN 900863, Baltimore, MD, May 2014, http://www.cms.gov/Outreach-and-Education/ Medicare-Learning-Network-MLN/MLNProducts/downloads/Section_1011_Fact_Sheet.pdf and CRS Report RL31630, Federal Funding for Unauthorized Aliens' Emergency Medical Expenses.

[102] CRS analysis of HHS annual "Budget in Brief" and congressional budget justification documents, http://dhhs.gov/ asfr/ob/docbudget; for more information about this program.

[103] U.S. Department of Health and Human Services, Assistant Secretary for Preparedness and Response, "Public Health Emergency/Hospital Preparedness Program (HPP)," July 16, 2014, http://www.phe.gov/PREPAREDNESS/ PLANNING/HPP/Pages/default.aspx.

[104] 42 U.S.C. §§1201-1246.

[105] U.S. Department of Health and Human Services, Centers for Disease Control and Prevention, "Injury Prevention and Control: Trauma Care," August 24, 2014, http://www.cdc.gov/traumacare/access_trauma.html.

[106] See, for example, descriptions of HRSA programs to support primary care in CRS Report R43177, Health Workforce Programs in Title VII of the Public Health Service Act, and U.S. Department of Health and Human Services, "National Health Service Corps," http://nhsc.hrsa.gov/. The National Health Service Corps provides scholarship and loan repayment to primary care and behavioral health providers, among others, who provide care in health professional shortage areas.

[107] CRS Report R42433, Federal Health Centers.

[108] U.S. Government Accountability Office, Hospital Emergency Departments: Health Center Strategies that May Help Reduce Their Use, GAO-11-414R, April 11, 2011.

[109] U.S. Department of Health and Human Services, Center for Medicare & Medicaid Services, Emergency Room Diversion Grant Program, Baltimore, MD, 2013, http://www.medicaid.gov/Medicaid-CHIP-Program-Information/ByTopics/Delivery-Systems/Grant-Programs/ER-Diversion-Grants.html.

[110] R.M. Coffey, Emergency Department Use for Mental Health and Substance Use Disorders, U.S. Agency for Healthcare Research and Quality (AHRQ), Rockville, MD, August 23, 2010, http://www.hcup-us.ahrq.gov/reports/ ED_Multivar_Rpt_Revision_Final072010.pdf.

[111] CRS Report R43681, SAMHSA FY2015 Budget Request and Funding History: A Fact Sheet.

[112] CRS Report R43255, The Mental Health Workforce: A Primer.

[113] Centers for Medicare and Medicaid Services, "Medicaid Emergency Psychiatric Demonstration," http://innovation.cms.gov/initiatives/medicaid-emergency-psychiatric-demo/.

[114] CRS Report R43328, Medicaid Coverage of Long-Term Services and Supports.

[115] National Alliance on Mental Illness, "Policy Topics: Background Information on IMD Exclusion," http://www.nami.org/Template.cfm?Section=Issue_Spotlights&template=/ ContentManagement/ContentDisplay.cfm& ContentID=44050.

[116] For more information, see "Federally Supported Care Coordination Models" in this report.

[117] CRS Report R41705, The National Institutes of Health (NIH): Background and Congressional Issues, by Judith A. Johnson.

[118] For more information, see National Institutes of Health, National Institute of General Medical Sciences, "Office of Emergency Care Research," September 8, 2014, http://www.nigms.nih.gov/About/Overview/OECR/Pages/ default.aspx.

[119] See, for example, National Institutes of Health, National Heart Lung and Blood Institute, Emergency Department Management of Acute Heart Failure: Research Challenges and Opportunities, Bethesda, MD, February 2010, http://www.nhlbi.nih.gov/research/ reports/ 2009-ed-mgmt-ahf.htm.

[120] Institute of Medicine of the National Academies, Hospital-Based Emergency Care: At the Breaking Point (Washington, DC: National Academies Press, 2006); Institute of Medicine of the National Academies, Emergency Medical Services: At the Crossroads (Washington, DC: National Academies Press, 2006); and Institute of Medicine of the National Academies, Hospital-Based Emergency Care for Children: Growing Pains (Washington, DC: National Academies Press, 2006).

[121] Brent R. Asplin et al., "A Conceptual Model of Emergency Department Crowding," Annals of Emergency Medicine, vol. 42, no. 2 (August 2003), pp. 173-180.

[122] Elaine Rabin et al., "Solutions to Emergency Department 'Boarding' and Crowding Are Underused and May Need to Be Legislated," Health Affairs, vol. 31, no. 8 (2012), pp.1757-1766. In some cases, hospital or ED inefficiencies cause or contribute to crowding. A number of the potential solutions presented below include hospital-level efficiencies that aim to reduce ED crowding. Still, in GAO's 2009 report, they noted that some hospitals have implemented strategies to reduce crowding, but that crowding persisted despite some hospital's efforts. See GAO-09-347.

[123] Marcus Ong Eng Hock et al., "Should Emergency Departments Be Society's Health Safety Net?" Journal of Public Health Policy, vol. 26, no. 3 (2005), pp. 269-281.

[124] GAO-09-347. In 2012, there were 575 fewer EDs than were available in 1992. See American Hospital Association, TrendWatch Chartbook 2014, Table 3.3 Emergency Department

Visits, Emergency Department Visits per 1,000 and Number of Emergency Departments, 1992-2012, http://www.aha.org/research/reports/tw/chartbook/index.shtml.

[125] GAO-09-347.

[126] Institute of Medicine (IOM) Hospital-Based Emergency Care: At the Breaking Point. National Academy of Sciences: Washington, DC, 2007.

[127] Ibid.

[128] GAO-09-34. Hospitals in MSAs also have high rates of nursing vacancies, which may increase their need to board patients, because they lack the nursing staff to care for additional inpatients. See, for example, Catharine W. Burt, and Linda F. McCaig, Centers for Disease Control and Prevention, National Center for Health Statistics, Staffing, Capacity, and Ambulance Diversion in Emergency Departments, Emergency Departments: United States, 2003–04, No. 376, Hyattsville, MD, September 27, 2006, http://www.cdc.gov/nchs/data/ad/ad376.pdf.

[129] Mark M. Moy, The EMTALA Answer Book: 2009 Edition (Wolters Kluwer Law & Business, 2009).

[130] Elaine Rabin et al., "Solutions to Emergency Department 'Boarding' and Crowding Are Underused and May Need to Be Legislated," Health Affairs, vol. 31, no. 8 (2012), pp.1757-1766.

[131] Brent R. Asplin et al., "A Conceptual Model of Emergency Department Crowding," Annals of Emergency Medicine, vol. 42, no. 2 (August 2003), pp. 173-180.

[132] Elaine Rabin et al., "Solutions to Emergency Department 'Boarding' and Crowding Are Underused and May Need to Be Legislated," Health Affairs, vol. 31, no. 8 (2012), pp.1757-1766. Despite public perceptions otherwise, inappropriate use is not a major contributor to crowding. See Adrian Boyle, et al., "Emergency Department Crowding: Time for Interventions and Policy Evaluations." Emergency Medicine International, Volume 2012, (2012). Hospitals face financial pressures to operate at or close to capacity; as such, they attempt to schedule elective surgical procedures to assure that most or all inpatient beds are full. See GAO-09-347.

[133] Catharine W. Burt, and Linda F. McCaig, Centers for Disease Control and Prevention, National Center for Health Statistics, Staffing, Capacity, and Ambulance Diversion in Emergency Departments, Emergency Departments: United States, 2003–04, No. 376, Hyattsville, MD, September 27, 2006, http://www.cdc.gov/nchs/data/ad/ad376.pdf.

[134] Elaine Rabin et al., "Solutions to Emergency Department 'Boarding' and Crowding Are Underused and May Need to Be Legislated," Health Affairs, vol. 31, no. 8 (2012), pp. 1757-1766.

[135] Ibid.

[136] Brent R. Asplin et al., "A Conceptual Model of Emergency Department Crowding," Annals of Emergency Medicine, vol. 42, no. 2 (August 2003), pp. 173-180.

[137] Ibid.

[138] Institute of Medicine (IOM) Hospital-Based Emergency Care: At the Breaking Point. National Academy of Sciences: Washington, DC, 2007.

[139] ED treatments are any treatments that patients require to treat their acute problem. Treatments are not necessarily activities, such as sutures or splint application; treatments also include consultations or a physician's decision to admit, transfer, or discharge. See, Brent R. Asplin et al., "A Conceptual Model of Emergency Department Crowding," Annals of Emergency Medicine, vol. 42, no. 2 (August 2003), pp. 173-180. Discharge refers to "discharge out of the ED" whether the discharge is to another hospital department, another facility, discharged to home, or death. See, GAO-09- 347.

[140] Stephen R. Pitts et al., "Where Americans Get Acute Care: Increasingly, It's Not at Their Doctor's Office." Health Affairs, vol. 29, no. 9 (September 2010), pp. 1620-1629.

[141] GAO-09-347.

[142] Government Accountability Office. (2003) Hospital Emergency Departments: Crowded Conditions Vary among Hospitals and Communities. GAO-03-460.

[143] For example, GAO found that hospitals' attempts to fill all inpatient beds contributes to crowding. See GAO-09- 347.

[144] Centers for Medicare & Medicaid Services, Extract of Final Report of the Emergency Medical Treatment and Labor Act Technical Advisory Group to the Secretary of the U.S. Department of Health and Human Services, Washington, DC, April 2, 2008, https://www.cms.gov/Regulations-and-Guidance/Legislation/EMTALA/downloads/ EMTALA_Final_Report_Summary.pdf.

[145] Elaine Rabin et al., "Solutions to Emergency Department 'Boarding' and Crowding Are Underused and May Need to Be Legislated," Health Affairs, vol. 31, no. 8 (2012), pp.1757-1766.

[146] Andrew A. Herring et al., "Increasing Critical Care Admissions from U.S. Emergency Departments, 2001-2009," Critical Care Medicine, vol. 41, no. 5 (May 2013), pp. 1197-1204 and Donald B. Chaflin et al., "Impact of Delayed Transfer of Critically Ill Patients from the Emergency Department to the Intensive Care Unit," Critical Care Medicine, vol. 35, no. 6 (June 2007), pp. 1477-1483.

[147] Not all ambulances are able to be diverted. If a patient requires immediate life sustaining treatment diversion requests are not honored.

[148] Nancy Stephens Donatelli, Jennifer Gregorwicz, and Joan Somes, "Extended ED Stay of the Older Adult Results in Poor Patient Outcomes," Journal of Emergency Nursing, vol. 39, no. 3 (May 2013), pp. 268-272.

[149] Elaine Rabin et al., "Solutions to Emergency Department 'Boarding' and Crowding Are Underused and May Need to Be Legislated," Health Affairs, vol. 31, no. 8 (2012), pp.1757-1766.

[150] Thomas Falvo et al., "The Opportunity Loss of Boarding Admitted Patients in the Emergency Department," Academic Emergency Medicine, vol. 14 (2007), pp. 332-337.

[151] Matthew Foley, Nizar Kifaieh, and William K. Mallon, "Financial Impact of Emergency Department Crowding," Western Journal of Emergency Medicine, vol. XII, no. 2 (May 2011), pp. 192-197.

[152] CRS Report R40425, Medicare Primer.

[153] Phillip L. Henneman et al., "Is Outpatient Emergency Department Care Profitable? Hourly Contribution Margins by Insurance for Patients Discharged From an Emergency Department," Annals of Emergency Medicine, vol. 63, no. 4 (April 2014), pp. 404-411.

[154] Centers for Medicare & Medicaid Services, Hospital Quality Initiative Overview, Baltimore, MD, July 2008, http://www.cms.gov/Medicare/Quality-Initiatives-Patient-Assessment-Instruments/HospitalQualityInits/Downloads/ HospitalOverview.pdf.

[155] CMS collects data that allows patients to compare a number of measures of hospital care, including those related to wait times in EDs, such as the time elapsed between when the patient enters the ED and receives a diagnostic evaluation and receives pain medication, if indicated. CMS also collects data on the number of patients who leave without being seen. See Centers for Medicare & Medicaid Services, "Data.Medicare.gov, Timely and Effective Care-Hospital," http://www.medicare.gov/hospitalcompare/About/Timely-Effective-Care. html. It is not clear the extent to which patients are using these data; however, applications are publicly available for patients to access these data. See, for example, Lena Groeger,

Mike Tigias, and Sisi Wei, "ER Wait Watcher: Which Emergency Room Will See You the Fastest?" at http://projects.propublica.org/emergency/.

[156] Centers for Medicare & Medicaid Services, Hospital Quality Initiative Overview, Baltimore, MD, July 2008, http://www.cms.gov/Medicare/Quality-Initiatives-Patient-Assessment-Instruments/HospitalQualityInits/Downloads/ HospitalOverview.pdf.

[157] Institute of Medicine of the National Academies, Hospital-Based Emergency Care: At the Breaking Point (Washington, DC: National Academies Press, 2006), p. 180.

[158] Adrian Boyle et al., "Emergency Department Crowding: Time for Interventions and Policy Evaluations." Emergency Medicine International, Volume 2012, (2012).

[159] Ben Wheatley, Rapporteur, Board on Health Care Services, Institute of Medicine, The National Emergency Care Enterprise: Advancing Care Through Collaboration: Workshop Summary (2009) (Washington, DC: The National Academies Press).

[160] Kent Rondeau and Louis Francescutti, "Emergency Department Overcrowding: The Impact of Resource Scarcity on Physician Job Satisfaction," Journal of Health Care Management, vol. 50, no. 5 (October 2005), pp. 327-340.

[161] Ben Wheatley, Rapporteur, Board on Health Care Services, Institute of Medicine, The National Emergency Care Enterprise: Advancing Care Through Collaboration: Workshop Summary (2009) (Washington, DC: The National Academies Press), p. 2009.

[162] Centers for Medicare & Medicaid Services, Office of the Actuary, National Health Statistics Group, National Health Expenditures Data, Baltimore, MD, 2012, http://www.cms.gov/Research-Statistics-Data-and-Systems/Statistics-Trends-and-Reports/NationalHealth ExpendData/Downloads/tables.pdf.

[163] Nancy Stephens Donatelli, Jennifer Gregorwicz, and Joan Somes, "Extended ED Stay of the Older Adult Results in Poor Patient Outcomes," Journal of Emergency Nursing, vol. 39, no. 3 (May 2013), pp. 268-272.

[164] Adverse events may be complications from being in a hospital, such as falls, or they may be more serious conditions that result from a delay in treatment, such as when delayed antibiotic administration leads to sepsis. In some instances, hospitals will not be paid by Medicare for conditions that Medicare patients acquire when hospitalized (i.e., for certain hospital-acquired conditions). See https://www.cms.gov/hospitalacqcond/06_hospital-acquired_conditions.asp.

[165] Unless otherwise specified, information in this section is from Elaine Rabin et al., "Solutions to Emergency Department 'Boarding' and Crowding Are Underused and May Need to Be Legislated," Health Affairs, vol. 31, no. 8 (2012), pp.1757-1766.

[166] David Mountain, "Introduction of a 4-hour rule in Western Australian Emergency Departments." Emergency Medicine Australasia, vol. 22 no. 5 (October 2010), pp. 374-378.

[167] Sally Gillen, "Quality Indicators Expected as Care Standard Is Relaxed." Emergency Nurse, vol. 18, no. 4: (2010), pp. 6-7.

[168] Social Security Act §1865; 42 U.S.C. §1395bb.

[169] For more information, see The Joint Commission, "Hospital Accreditation," http://www.jointcommission.org/ accreditation/hospitals.aspx.

[170] The Joint Commission, "Patient Flow Resources, The "Patient Flow Standard" and the 4-Hour Recommendation," http://www.jointcommission.org/accreditation/ patient_flow_ resources _.aspx.

[171] Elaine Rabin et al., "Solutions to Emergency Department 'Boarding' and Crowding Are Underused and May Need to Be Legislated," Health Affairs, vol. 31, no. 8 (2012), pp. 1757-1766.

[172] Frequent users are also called "super utilizers"; these terms are used interchangeably in this report.

[173] John Billings and Maria C. Raven, "Dispelling an Urban Legend: Frequent Emergency Department Users Have Substantial Burden of Disease," Health Affairs, vol. 32, no. 12 (December 2013), pp. 2099-2108.

[174] Ibid.

[175] However some frequent users share similarities such as being in poor health and having chronic conditions. A subset of frequent users are also disabled; among those with 15 or more annual ED visits, nearly two-thirds had a history of serious mental illness and substance use. See Medicaid and CHIP Payment Advisory Commission, MAC Facts, Key Findings on Medicaid and CHIP: Revisiting Emergency Department Use in Medicaid, Washington, DC, July 2014.

[176] Washington State Health Care Authority. Report to the Legislature: Emergency Department Utilization: Update on Assumed Savings from Best Practices Implementation. March 2014, http://www.hca.wa.gov/Documents/ EmergencyDeptUtilization.pdf.

[177] Anika Hines et al., Conditions with the Largest Number of Adult Hospital Readmissions by Payer, 2001, U.S. Department of Health and Human Services, Agency for Healthcare Research and Quality, Healthcare Cost and Utilization Project Statistical Brief #172, http://www.hcup-us.ahrq.gov/reports/statbriefs/sb172-ConditionsReadmissions-Payer.pdf.

[178] For example, some state Medicaid programs have chosen to use their Medicaid data systems to track frequent users and have received federal matching funds to support necessary data enhancements. This program is authorized in Sec. 1903(a)(3) of the Social Security Act.

[179] Unless otherwise noted, this paragraph is drawn from Letter from Cindy Mann, Director, Center for Medicaid and CHIP Services, "Targeting Medicaid Super-Utilizers to Decrease Costs and Improve Quality," July 24, 2013, http://medicaid.gov/Federal-Policy-Guidance/Downloads/CIB-07-24-2013.pdf.

[180] Patients may also be targeted for inclusion in super utilizer programs because they have frequent ED visits, are referred to the program by medical personnel, they have costly underlying medical conditions (e.g., cancer), or they have sociodemographic characteristics consistent with high use, among others.

[181] Some state Medicaid programs have also tried to reduce ED use by instituting copayments for non-emergency ED use. The effects of these copayments on reducing ED use are mixed because it is difficult to identify non-emergency use prospectively. See Medicaid and CHIP Payment Advisory Commission, MAC Facts, Key Findings on Medicaid and CHIP: Revisiting Emergency Department Use in Medicaid, Washington, DC, July 2014.

[182] ACOs (Shared Savings Program) were established in Section 1899; (42 U.S.C. §1395jjj of the Social Security Act (SSA)). See CMS, "What's an ACO?" http://www.cms.gov/Medicare/Medicare-Fee-for-Service-Payment/ACO/ index.html?redirect=/ACO.

[183] Centers for Medicare & Medicaid Services, "Bundled Payments for Care Improvement (BCPI) Initiative: General Information," http://innovation.cms.gov/initiatives/bundled-payments/.

[184] CRS Report R42941, Medicaid's Federal Medical Assistance Percentage (FMAP), FY2014.

[185] See ACA Sec. 2703 described in CRS Report R41210, Medicaid and the State Children's Health Insurance Program (CHIP) Provisions in ACA: Summary and Timeline. For states that focus care on Medicaid-Medicare enrollees, the Medicare Medicaid Coordination Office (MMCO) provides data access and free Medicare assistance.

[186] This program is authorized in SSA Sec. 1915(g) (42 U.S.C. §1396m). For more information, see Letter from Cindy Mann, Director Center for Medicaid and CHIP Services, "Targeting

Medicaid Super-Utilizers to Decrease Costs and Improve Quality," July 24, 2013, http://medicaid.gov/Federal-Policy-Guidance/Downloads/CIB-07-24-2013.pdf.

[187] R.M. Coffey, Emergency Department Use for Mental Health and Substance Use Disorders, U.S. Agency for Healthcare Research and Quality (AHRQ), Rockville, MD, August 23, 2010, http://www.hcup-us.ahrq.gov/reports/ ED_Multivar_Rpt_Revision_Final072010.pdf.

[188] Peter J. Cunningham, Kelly McKenzie, and Erin Fries Taylor, "The Struggle to Provide Community-Based Care to Low-Income People with Serious Mental Illness." Health Affairs, vol. 25, no.3 (2006), pp. 694-705.

[189] R.M. Coffey, Emergency Department Use for Mental Health and Substance Use Disorders, U.S. Agency for Healthcare Research and Quality (AHRQ), Rockville, MD, August 23, 2010, http://www.hcup-us.ahrq.gov/reports/ ED_Multivar_Rpt_Revision_Final072010.pdf.

[190] Ibid.

[191] CRS Insight IN10032, U.S. Opioid Epidemic: The Role of Heroin.

[192] R.M. Coffey, Emergency Department Use for Mental Health and Substance Use Disorders, U.S. Agency for Healthcare Research and Quality (AHRQ), Rockville, MD, August 23, 2010, http://www.hcup-us.ahrq.gov/reports/ ED_Multivar_Rpt_Revision_Final072010.pdf.

[193] Centers for Medicare & Medicaid Services, Extract of Final Report of the Emergency Medical Treatment and Labor Act Technical Advisory Group to the Secretary of the U.S. Department of Health and Human Services, Washington, DC, April 2, 2008, https://www.cms.gov/Regulations-and-Guidance/Legislation/EMTALA/downloads/ EMTALA_Final_Report_Summary.pdf.

[194] Peter J. Cunningham, Kelly McKenzie, and Erin Fries Taylor, "The Struggle to Provide Community-Based Care to Low-Income People with Serious Mental Illness." Health Affairs, vol. 25, no.3 (2006), pp. 694-705.

[195] See discussion in Anne Manton, Care of the Psychiatric Patient in the Emergency Department, Emergency Nurses Association, white paper, Des Plaines, IL, February 2013, http://www.ena.org/practice-research/research/Documents/ WhitePaperCareofPsych.pdf, p. 1.

[196] Lisa A. Wolf, Altair M. Delao, and Cydne Perhats, "Nothing Changes, Nobody Cares: Understanding the Experience of Emergency Nurses Physically or Verbally Assaulted While Providing Care," Journal of Emergency Nursing, vol. 40, no. 4 (July 2014), pp. 305-310; and Anne Manton, Care of the Psychiatric Patient in the Emergency Department, Emergency Nurses Association, white paper, Des Plaines, IL, February 2013, http://www.ena.org/ practice-research/research/Documents/WhitePaperCareofPsych.pdf.

[197] R.M. Coffey, Emergency Department Use for Mental Health and Substance Use Disorders, U.S. Agency for Healthcare Research and Quality (AHRQ), Rockville, MD, August 23, 2010, http://www.hcup-us.ahrq.gov/reports/ ED_Multivar_Rpt_Revision_Final072010.pdf.

[198] Certain plans that existed prior to the ACA are not subject to these requirements; see CRS Report R43048, Overview of Private Health Insurance Provisions in the Patient Protection and Affordable Care Act (ACA).

[199] CRS Report R41768, Mental Health Parity and Mandated Coverage of Mental Health and Substance Use Disorder Services After the ACA.

[200] Ibid.

[201] See discussion of mental health professional shortage areas in CRS Report R43255, The Mental Health Workforce: A Primer.

[202] GAO-09-347.

[203] For more information, see The Joint Commission, "Hospital Accreditation," http://www.jointcommission.org/ accreditation/hospitals.aspx.

[204] Social Security Act §1865; 42 U.S.C. §1395bb.

[205] The Joint Commission, "Patient Flow Resources, "The 'Patient Flow Standard' and the 4-Hour Recommendation," http://www.jointcommission.org/accreditation/ patient_flow_ resources_.aspx.

[206] For more information about the effect of elective surgery scheduling on ED boarding, see Elaine Rabin et al., "Solutions to Emergency Department 'Boarding' and Crowding Are Underused and May Need to Be Legislated," Health Affairs, vol. 31, no. 8 (2012), pp.1757-1766.

[207] CMS, "Medicare and Medicaid Programs; Emergency Preparedness Requirements for Medicare and Medicaid Participating Providers and Suppliers," 78 Federal Register 79082, December 27, 2013.

[208] 42 C.F.R. §440.255 "Limited services available to certain aliens."

[209] Centers for Medicare & Medicaid Services, Extract of Final Report of the Emergency Medical Treatment and Labor Act Technical Advisory Group to the Secretary of the U.S. Department of Health and Human Services, Washington, DC, April 2, 2008, https://www.cms.gov/Regulations-and-Guidance/Legislation/EMTALA/downloads/ EMTALA_Final_Report_Summary.pdf. The ACA authorized a program that would provide funding to trauma centers based on the amount of uncompensated care that its ED provides. This program has not received appropriations; if appropriations were to be made available, the program would not provide funds to EDs that do not have trauma centers. For more information about this program, see CRS Report R41278, Public Health, Workforce, Quality, and Related Provisions in ACA: Summary and Timeline.

[210] U.S. Department of Health and Human Services, Centers for Medicare & Medicaid Services, Emergency Room Diversion Grant Program, Baltimore, MD, 2013, http://www.medicaid. gov/Medicaid-CHIP-Program-Information/ByTopics/Delivery-Systems/Grant-Programs/ER-Diversion-Grants.html.

[211] Kristy Gonzalez Morganti et al., "The State of Innovative Emergency Medical Service Programs in the United States," Prehospital Emergency Care, vol. 18, no. 1 (January/March 2014), pp. 76-85.

[212] Ibid.

[213] National Alliance on Mental Illness, "Policy Topics: Background Information on IMD Exclusion," http://www.nami.org/Template.cfm?Section=Issue_Spotlights&template=/ ContentManagement/ContentDisplay.cfm& ContentID=44050.

[214] Ibid and CRS Report R43328, Medicaid Coverage of Long-Term Services and Supports, by Kirsten J. Colello.

[215] Ibid.

[216] Anna Gorman, "Urgent Care Centers Opening for People with Mental Illness," Capsules: The KHN Blog, August 28, 2014.

[217] For more information, see CRS Report R42433, Federal Health Centers.

[218] Barbara Y. DiPietro, Dana Kindermann, and Stephen M. Schenkel, "Ill, Itinerant, and Insured; The Top 20 Users of Emergency Departments in Baltimore City," The Scientific World Journal, vol. 2012 (2012).

[219] For more information, see National Institutes of Health, National Institute of General Medical Sciences, "Office of Emergency Care Research," September 8, 2014, http:// www.nigms.nih.gov/About/Overview/OECR/Pages/ default.aspx.

[220] Section 1251 of the Public Health Service Act authorizes funding for residency training in emergency medicine; authorization for these grants expired in FY2012 and this program is not currently funded. In addition, the ACA authorized a program to train physicians in

trauma care, which is more specific than emergency care. For a description of this program, see CRS Report R41278, Public Health, Workforce, Quality, and Related Provisions in ACA: Summary and Timeline.

[221] Adrian Boyle, et al., "Emergency Department Crowding: Time for Interventions and Policy Evaluations." Emergency Medicine International, Volume 2012, (2012).

[222] For more information and measures, see Centers for Medicare & Medicaid Services, "Data.Medicare.gov, Timely and Effective Care-Hospital," http://www.medicare.gov/hospitalcompare/About/Timely-Effective-Care.html.

[223] A number of state laws also regulate emergency care.

[224] Section 945 of the Medicare Prescription Drug, Improvement, and Modernization Act of 2003 (P.L. 108-173) required the HHS Secretary to establish a technical advisory group (TAG) to advise the Secretary about issues related to the regulation and implementation of EMTALA. The group's charter expired in 2007.

[225] Unless otherwise noted, this list is drawn from Centers for Medicare & Medicaid Services, Extract of Final Report of the Emergency Medical Treatment and Labor Act Technical Advisory Group to the Secretary of the U.S. Department of Health and Human Services, Washington, DC, April 2, 2008, https://www.cms.gov/Regulations-andGuidance/Legislation/EMTALA/downloads/EMTALA_Final_Report_Summary.pdf.

[226] Some facilities have instituted policies that place ED boarding patients in the hallways of inpatient units; although this is not an ideal solution, it frees up ED resources to receive incoming ambulances, and the patients who are boarded in the inpatient unit receive care from inpatient care staff. For more information, see Elaine Rabin et al., "Solutions to Emergency Department 'Boarding' and Crowding Are Underused and May Need to Be Legislated," Health Affairs, vol. 31, no. 8 (2012), pp.1757-1766.

In: Hospital Emergency Departments
Editor: Daniel T. Lee
ISBN: 978-1-63482-170-4

Chapter 2

EMTALA: ACCESS TO EMERGENCY MEDICAL CARE*

Edward C. Liu

SUMMARY

The Emergency Medical Treatment and Active Labor Act (EMTALA) ensures universal access to emergency medical care at all Medicare participating hospitals with emergency departments. Under EMTALA, any person who seeks emergency medical care at a covered facility, regardless of ability to pay, immigration status, or any other characteristic, is guaranteed an appropriate screening exam and stabilization treatment before transfer or discharge. Failure to abide by these requirements can subject hospitals or physicians to civil monetary sanctions or exclusion from Medicare. Hospitals, but not physicians, may also be sued by private individuals who suffer personal injuries as a result of a violation of EMTALA.

A dispute over the interpretation of the statute has recently arisen in the context of the application of EMTALA to individuals who come to a hospital emergency room and are subsequently admitted to the hospital as inpatients. Regulations promulgated by the Centers for Medicare and Medicaid Services (CMS) have taken the position that a hospital's EMTALA obligations end once an individual is admitted as an inpatient.

* This is an edited, reformatted and augmented version of a Congressional Research Service publication RS22738, prepared for Members and Committees of Congress dated December 28, 2010.

However, in *Moses v. Providence Hospital*, the United States Court of Appeals for the Sixth Circuit held that, despite these regulations, transferring or discharging an *inpatient* without stabilizing an emergency medical condition could still constitute a violation of EMTALA. Consequently, a hospital's obligations to inpatients under EMTALA may be modulated by the *Moses* decision if the hospital happens to be located in the Sixth Circuit's jurisdiction (Kentucky, Michigan, Ohio, and Tennessee).

In December of 2010, CMS solicited comments on whether CMS's inpatient regulations should be revisited. The solicited comments may provide specific examples of individuals' treatment after being admitted from the emergency room, which may be of interest to both agency officials and legislators.

In 1986, Congress enacted the Emergency Medical Treatment and Active Labor Act (EMTALA)[1] to address the problem of "patient dumping" in hospital emergency departments. Patient dumping refers to instances in which a hospital turns away indigent or uninsured persons seeking treatment so that the hospital will not have to absorb the cost of treating them. Although attempts to facilitate indigent access to emergency health care already existed in state and federal law, legal frameworks prior to EMTALA were plagued with poor enforcement mechanisms and vague standards of conduct.[2] Amid graphic media reports of hospitals sending away critically ill patients without proper stabilization treatment and delivery rooms unwilling to accept indigent or uninsured women in labor, Congress passed EMTALA as part of the Consolidated Omnibus Budget Reconciliation Act of 1985.[3]

EMTALA's statutory scheme has traditionally been deconstructed into two principal categories: (1) provisions that ensure an appropriate medical screening, and (2) provisions that require stabilization before transfer or discharge.[4] EMTALA only requires stabilization of whatever emergency conditions a hospital detects, and does not provide a right to indefinite care for anyone who comes to an emergency room. EMTALA's requirements may be suspended by the Secretary of Health and Human Services during national emergencies, such as the recent landfall of Hurricane Ike in Texas.[5] Hospitals and physicians that fail to comply with these requirements may be fined $50,000 and/or excluded from participation in Medicare, and hospitals may also be held civilly liable to persons who suffer personal injury.[6]

The Screening Requirement

Only hospitals that (1) participate in Medicare and (2) maintain an emergency department are required to screen patients under EMTALA.[7] Hospitals that do not have a "dedicated emergency department" are not subject to the screening requirement of EMTALA.[8] Similarly, emergency care providers that are unaffiliated with a hospital need not comply with EMTALA, even where those providers are the only medical care facilities reasonably accessible.9 For example, in Rodriguez v. American Int'l Ins. Co. of Puerto Rico, the First Circuit declined to extend EMTALA protections to a 24-hour emergency room clinic in rural Puerto Rico because the clinic was not associated with a hospital. The Federal District Court for the District of Puerto Rico had initially held that, because the clinic was the primary provider of 24-hour emergency health care in its area, applying EMTALA to the clinic best furthered the statutory goal of universal access to emergency medical care.10 However, the First Circuit reversed, holding that any considerations of the goals of Congress were inappropriate where the text of the statute was clear.[11]

When Is the Screening Requirement Triggered?

The screening requirement is triggered when an individual "comes to the emergency department" of a hospital and requests to be treated.[12] Under HHS regulations, an individual may be deemed to have come to the emergency department in certain circumstances, even though the individual is not physically present in the emergency department or elsewhere on the hospital campus.[13] For example, a patient en-route to a hospital in an ambulance or air transport owned by that hospital has "come to the emergency department" of that hospital and may not be refused a screening exam under EMTALA. These regulations also state that incoming patients in ambulances that are not owned by the receiving hospital have not "come to the emergency department." The regulations further allow the hospital to redirect the non-owned ambulance if the hospital is in "diversionary status."[14] However, at least one Federal Court of Appeal has rejected this interpretation of the statute and has held that EMTALA could be triggered by an incoming ambulance that was not owned by the receiving hospital.[15]

In *Morales v. Sociedad Espanola*, the hospital had argued that HHS regulations clearly state that patients in non-owned ambulances have not yet "come to the emergency department," and therefore EMTALA did not apply. However, according to the First Circuit's reading of the pertinent regulations, a hospital is only permitted to take the *affirmative action* of refusing a non-owned ambulances if it is actually in "diversionary status." The court argued that this reading gives effect to every word in the regulation and also best effectuates EMTALA's statutory goal of preventing patient dumping.[16]

Regardless of whether the ambulance is owned by a hospital or not, should an ambulance ignore a redirection request, EMTALA is triggered if the patient physically arrives on the hospital's property.[17]

What Constitutes an "Appropriate Screening Exam"?

Although hospitals with dedicated emergency departments are required to perform screening exams, it is not necessarily a violation of EMTALA if a screening exam falls short of either a local or national medical malpractice standard.[18] The language of the statute requires only "an appropriate medical screening exam."[19] The majority of the federal circuits have held that, because the chief evil sought to be prevented was the lack of access for uninsured patients, an "appropriate" exam is one comparable to what a paying patient would receive under similar circumstances.[20] However, the Sixth Circuit has construed the statute more narrowly, holding that there is no violation of EMTALA without the additional allegation of an "improper motive" that led to a substandard screening exam.[21]

THE STABILIZATION REQUIREMENT

Like the screening requirement, the stabilization requirement applies to all Medicare participating hospitals with a dedicated emergency department. However, in some cases the stabilization requirement may also apply to a Medicare participating hospital even if it does not have an emergency department. For example, if treatment of an individual's medical condition requires a particular hospital's unique equipment or expertise, federal regulations compel that hospital to accept a transfer of that patient from any nearby U.S. hospital.[22]

The stabilization requirement is triggered when a hospital discovers that an individual has an emergency medical condition. Actual knowledge of an emergency medical condition is required.[23] Therefore, if a hospital fails to accurately detect an individual's emergency condition and discharges that individual without stabilizing the medical condition, the hospital may not have violated EMTALA's stabilization provisions. However, the hospital may still be civilly liable to the individual based upon state medical malpractice claims if the failure to detect an emergency condition was due to negligence during the screening exam.[24]

Interpretations of the Stabilization Requirement

Except where medically necessary, hospitals must ensure that an individual is stabilized before discharge or transfer. Federal regulations define an individual as stabilized as either (1) when there is a reasonable assurance that no material deterioration would result from that individual's transfer or discharge from the hospital or, (2) in the case of women in labor, after delivery of the child and placenta.[25] Unlike the screening requirement, the language of the stabilization requirement does not qualify the care to be given as "appropriate."[26] Based on this textual distinction, the U.S. Supreme Court has held that no "improper motive" need be alleged to show a violation of EMTALA's stabilization provisions.[27]

Stabilization and Inpatient Status

When an emergency medical condition is detected, a hospital may decide to admit the individual as an inpatient for further treatment. Whether the stabilization requirement continues to apply to patients after they have been admitted is a disputed issue. Because the statute only defines "stabilization" in the context of transfers, the Fourth, Ninth and Eleventh Circuits have held that a hospital has no stabilization duties that are enforceable under EMTALA once an individual has been admitted.[28] However, the Sixth Circuit[29] had held otherwise in *Thornton v. Southwest Detroit Hospital*.[30] In that case, a stroke victim alleged she was discharged from the ICU without being stabilized, in violation of EMTALA, after 21 days of inpatient care. The Sixth Circuit held that EMTALA still required stabilization before discharge, despite her inpatient status.[31]

Despite this split in circuit authority, the Supreme Court declined to rule on this issue in *Roberts v. Galen*, although it had an opportunity to do so.[32]

During oral arguments for that case, the office of the Solicitor General, arguing as amicus curiae, informed the Court that the Department of Health and Human Services intended to begin rule-making procedures to provide guidance on this question.[33] In 2002, the Centers for Medicare and Medicaid Services (CMS) issued a notice of a proposed rule extending EMTALA protections to inpatients.[34] Many comments noted the *Bryant v. Adventist*[35] decision holding otherwise,[36] and in 2003, CMS reversed its position, stating that if, after performing a screening exam, a hospital admits an individual for treatment of an emergency medical condition, then the hospital has satisfied its duties under EMTALA.[37]

In August of 2008, HHS further clarified its position by stating that EMTALA does not apply to an individual who has been screened and admitted at one hospital but requires a transfer to a second hospital that has specialized facilities.[38] As described above, where a patient has not yet been admitted, nearby specialized hospitals are generally required to accept transfers of the patient from the original hospital.[39] However, the new regulations clearly state that once the individual has been admitted as an inpatient in one hospital, other specialized hospitals do not continue to have a duty to accept a transfer under EMTALA.[40]

Despite the promulgation of these rules, the Sixth Circuit has continued to hold that the mere admission of an individual, without further treatment, does not satisfy EMTALA.[41] In *Moses v. Providence Hospital*, the court found CMS's regulations to be contrary to the plain language of the statute. Therefore, the regulations were not entitled to deference.[42] In particular, the court relied upon language in EMTALA which prohibits hospitals from releasing patients with emergency medical conditions without providing treatment to stabilize the condition. According to the court, the CMS regulations would permit hospitals to avoid EMTALA liability by simply admitting and immediately discharging patients, without providing any treatment. The court found such a construction to be unreasonable and contrary to the language of the statute.[43] However, one could argue that by admitting an individual, a hospital is subject to potential medical malpractice liability under state law. Therefore, while the CMS regulations may provide a means of avoiding EMTALA liability by admitting and discharging individuals, compliance with CMS's interpretation would not necessarily immunize hospitals from applicable state law claims. Insofar as the intent of EMTALA was to prevent situations in which hospitals could "dump" patients without incurring any liability, providing an incentive for hospitals to admit emergency room patients may be consistent with that goal. Once a patient is admitted, it could be argued that EMTALA liability is unnecessary as state medical malpractice law could provide an incentive for the hospital to ensure the provision of necessary stabilizing treatment.

The defendant hospital in *Moses* petitioned the Supreme Court for review, but the Court declined to hear the case.[44] This would appear to indicate that a split of circuit authority remains with respect to EMTALA's application to admitted persons. However, it should be noted that the Sixth Circuit's decision in *Moses* also relied on the fact that the underlying hospital visit occurred in 2002 before CMS had promulgated its regulations on inpatient status. Additionally, the Court noted that CMS's regulations did not expressly indicate an intent to apply retroactively. Furthermore, presuming retroactive application would have adversely affected the patient's expectations at the time care was sought, based on the Sixth Circuit's earlier decision in *Thornton.* Because of these considerations, the Sixth Circuit held, in the alternative, that even if CMS's interpretation of the statute was entitled to deference in prospective cases, it should not be given retroactive effect to the specific facts before it.[45] However, despite these alternative grounds, at least one federal district court in the Sixth Circuit has cited *Moses* for the proposition that "EMTALA [currently] imposes an obligation on a hospital beyond simply admitting a patient with an emergency medical condition to an inpatient care unit."[46]

In December of 2010, CMS issued an advance notice of proposed rulemaking and solicited comments regarding whether it should revisit its regulations which provide that a hospital's EMTALA obligations end once a patient has been admitted.[47] In its request for comment, CMS specifically requested "real world examples" and comments that described situations where an admitted emergency room patient was subsequently transferred despite the admitting hospital's ability to treat the patient's condition.[48]

Stabilization of Known Emergency Conditions

The stabilization requirement may preempt certain state laws authorizing physicians to decline administering treatment where deemed inappropriate based upon their medical judgment. In *re Baby K*, a hospital sought a declaratory judgment that they were permitted to refuse to treat an anencephalic infant in respiratory distress.[49] The hospital argued that the prevailing standard of care for anencephalic infants was to provide warmth and nutrition without mechanical respiration, and that Virginia state law authorized physicians to refuse to provide care they believed would be inappropriate.[50] The Fourth Circuit disagreed and held that the requirement of stabilization prior to transfer or discharge was compulsory once an emergency medical condition had been identified by hospital personnel, even where the treating physician believed stabilization treatment would have been futile. Furthermore, the court held that EMTALA preempted the Virginia statute authorizing the physician to refuse to provide treatment he reasonably believed to be inappropriate.[51]

Requirements for Transfers after Stabilization

All transfers must be conducted with qualified personnel and equipment. An individual may not be transferred unless the receiving hospital consents to receive the individual. The receiving hospital must have the capacity and expertise to treat the transferred individual, and all medical records must be sent to the receiving hospital. It is the transferring hospital's obligation to ensure that the transfer has been performed as described above and the transferring hospital remains liable under EMTALA until an appropriate transfer is completed.[52] It is not a violation of EMTALA to transfer an individual who has not been stabilized when it is medically necessary to do so. In such situations, a qualified medical person, as defined by the hospital's own rules and regulations, must certify that the benefits of transfer to a different facility outweigh the risks involved.[53]

HOSPITAL LIABILITY TO THIRD PARTIES

EMTALA provides a civil remedy to "any individual who suffers personal harm as a direct result of a participating hospital's violation." In 2009, the Sixth Circuit held that this language provided a civil remedy to third parties that were injured as a direct result of a violation of either the screening or stabilization requirements.[54] In the case before the court, the hospital was alleged to have improperly discharged an emergency room patient who was psychiatrically unstable. Ten days after his discharge the patient murdered his wife. The wife's estate subsequently brought suit against the hospital alleging that the hospital's failure to stabilize before discharge was a direct cause of her death. The defendants argued that the patient's wife lacked standing under EMTALA because it only permitted civil claims by persons that were personally denied treatment in violation of the statute. In support of this argument, the defendants noted that, during consideration of EMTALA, the House Judiciary Committee had issued a report stating

> [The civil suit provision of EMTALA] authorizes only two types of actions for damages. The first of these could be brought by the individual patient who suffers harm as a direct result of [a] hospital's failure to appropriately screen, stabilize, or properly transfer that patient. The second type of action could be brought by a medical facility which received an improperly transferred emergency patient.[55]

Because third parties were not mentioned in the legislative history, the defendants argued that this suit should not be permitted. The Sixth Circuit disagreed, noting that

> where a House committee's explanation of the meaning of a statute seems to differ from the statute's actual wording, this Court should not rely on that committee's statement as the exclusive explanation for the meaning of the statute.... We recognize that our interpretation of the civil enforcement provision may have consequences for hospitals that Congress may or may not have considered or intended. However, our duty is only to read the statute as it is written.[56]

In the court's view, the statutory text afforded a civil remedy to "*any* individual who suffers personal harm as a direct result" of the hospital's actions, and the most logical reading of this text permits suits to be brought by harmed third parties.[57]

End Notes

[1] P.L. 99-272, 100 Stat. 164 (1986) codified at 42 U.S.C. § 1395dd et seq. (2007).

[2] Tiana Mayere Lee, An EMTALA Primer: The Impact of Changes in the Emergency Medicine Landscape on EMTALA Compliance and Enforcement, 13 ANNALS OF HEALTH L. 145, 146-147 (2004) (discussing the Hill-Burton Act and state statutory and common law). See also H.Rept. 99-241, pt. 3, at 5 (1985) (discussing state remedies).

[3] Lee, supra note 2 at 147-148, 151.

[4] 42 U.S.C. § 1395dd(a), (b).

[5] 42 U.S.C. § 1320b-5(b)(3). See Waiver or Modification of Requirements Under Section 1135 of the Social Security Act, Michael O. Leavitt, Secretary of the Department of Health and Human Services, (Sept. 11, 2008), available at http://www.hhs.gov/disasters/emergency/naturaldisasters/hurricanes/ike/1135waiver.html. Sanctions are only lifted for inappropriate transfers or redirections. 42 C.F.R. § 489.24(a)(2).

[6] 42 U.S.C. § 1395dd(d). Civil fines are limited to $25,000 for hospitals with fewer than 100 beds. Id. at (d)(1)(A). Private suits may not be brought against physicians individually. See e.g. Heimlicher v. Steele, 442 F. Supp. 2d 685 (N.D. Iowa 2006) (citing King v. Ahrens, 16

F.3d 265 (8th Cir. 1994), Delaney v. Cade, 986 F.2d 387 (10th Cir. 1993), and Baber v. Hosp. Corp. of Am., 977 F.2d 872 (4th Cir. 1992)). Medicare termination appears to be infrequently invoked as a sanction. Laura D. Hermer, The Scapegoat: EMTALA and Emergency Department Overcrowding, 14 J. L. & Policy 695, 701 n. 29 (2006) (stating that between 1986 and 2001 only four hospitals had their Medicare agreements terminated).

[7] 42 U.S.C. § 1395dd(a), (d)(1)(A), and (e)(2). Although the screening and stabilization requirements are phrased such that they apply to "hospitals" generally, enforcement of EMTALA is only authorized against hospitals that have entered into a Medicare provider agreement. Id.

[8] 42 U.S.C. § 1395dd(a). A dedicated emergency department is defined as any facility that is licensed or held out to the public as such, or that provides urgent care to one third of its outpatients during the preceding calendar year. 42 C.F.R. § 489.24(b).

[9] Rodriguez v. American Int'l Ins. Co. of Puerto Rico, 402 F.3d 45 (1st Cir. 2005).

[10] Rodriguez v. American Int'l Ins. Co. of Puerto Rico, 263 F. Supp. 2d 297 (D. Puerto Rico 2003) (arguing that the nature of the services provided should be determinative, not whether a facility is defined as a hospital).

[11] Rodriguez v. American Int'l, 402 F.3d at 49 (noting that Congress was free in drafting the statute to extend EMTALA to rural clinics unaffiliated with hospitals, but had not done so). EMTALA does apply to facilities designated as "critical access hospitals," which provide 24-hour emergency services and acute inpatient care to rural areas. 42 U.S.C. § 1395dd(e)(5).

[12] 42 U.S.C. § 1395dd(a). Requests for treatment may be made on the individual's behalf and a request may be implied if a prudent layperson observer would believe that the individual needs emergency medical care. 42 C.F.R. § 489.24(b) (2006).

[13] 42 C.F.R. § 489.24(b). The campus includes areas within 250 yards of a hospital's main buildings. 42 C.F.R. § 413.65(b).

[14] 42 C.F.R. § 489.24(b). A hospital is in diversionary status if it lacks the staff or facilities to treat additional emergency patients. See also Arrington v. Wong, 237 F.3d 1066, 1072 (9th Cir. 2001) (reasoning through negative implication that a hospital may not divert an ambulance if it is not in diversionary status).

[15] Morales v. Sociedad Española de Auxilio Mutuo y Beneficencia, 524 F.3d 54 (1st Cir. 2008) (cert. denied Sociedad Espanola v. Morales, 77 U.S.LW. 3396 (2009)).

[16] Id. at 59-62.

[17] 42 C.F.R. § 489.24(b). Prior to the promulgation of these regulations, the Seventh Circuit had held that contacting a hospital via telemetry alone does not invoke EMTALA. Johnson v. Univ. of Chicago Hosps., 982 F.2d 230 (7th Cir. 1993). These regulations are consonant with that holding.

[18] Phillips v. Hillcrest Med. Ctr., 244 F.3d 790 (10th Cir. 2001) (noting that EMTALA was not enacted to create a federal medical malpractice standard).

[19] 42 U.S.C. § 1395dd(a). Screening exams may vary based upon a hospital's capabilities and the nature of an individual's request. 42 C.F.R. § 489.24(a)(i) and (c).

[20] Correa v. Hosp. San Francisco, 69 F.3d 1184 (1st Cir. 1995), Baber v. Hosp. Corp. of America, 977 F.2d 872 (4th Cir. 1992), Marshall v. E. Carroll Parish Hosp. Serv., 134 F.3d 319 (5th Cir. 1998), Summers v. Baptist Med. Ctr. Arkadelphia, 91 F.3d 1132 (8th Cir. 1996), Jackson v. E. Bay Hosp., 246 F.3d 1248 (9th Cir. 2001), Holcomb v. Monahan, 30 F.3d 116 (11th Cir. 1994), Gatewood v. Wash. Healthcare Corp., 933 F.2d 1037 (D. C. Cir. 1991).

[21] Cleland v. Bronson Health Care Group, Inc., 917 F2d 266, 272 (6th Cir. 1990). Gender, race, nationality, financial insolvency, bias against a particular medical condition, and personal animosity were examples of improper motivation offered by the Cleland court.

[22] 42 C.F.R. § 489.24(f). Examples of specialized equipment or expertise include burn units, shock-trauma units, neonatal intensive care units, or regional referral centers.

[23] 42 U.S.C. § 1395dd(b)(1) and 42 C.F.R. § 489.24(a)(1)(ii).

[24] Bryant v. Adventist, infra note 28 at 1166.

[25] 42 C.F.R. § 489.24(b).

[26] 42 U.S.C. § 1395dd(b)(1)(A).

[27] Roberts v. Galen, 525 U.S. 249, 252-3 (1999). The Court expressly declined to decide whether the "improper motive" requirement was required with respect to EMTALA's screening provisions. Id. at 253 n.1. See also supra notes 20-21 and accompanying text.

[28] Bryan v. Rectors & Visitors of the Univ. of Virginia, 95 F.3d 349, 352 (4th Cir. 1996), Bryant v. Adventist Health Sys., 289 F.3d 1162, 1168-1169 (9th Cir. 2002), Harry v. Marchant, 291 F.3d 767 (11th Cir. 2002).

[29] The Sixth Circuit Court of Appeals has jurisdiction over appeals from federal courts in Kentucky, Michigan, Ohio, and Tennessee.

[30] Thornton v. Southwest Detroit Hosp., 895 F.2d 1131, 1135 (6th Cir. 1990).

[31] The Sixth Circuit argued in dictum that if EMTALA did not apply to inpatients, hospitals could avoid EMTALA liability by admitting, and immediately discharging, a patient. Id. at 1135.

[32] Roberts v. Galen, 525 U.S. at 253-4 n.2.

[33] Transcript of Oral Argument at 17-20, Roberts v. Galen, supra note 27. The Solicitor General also argued that the question of inpatient status had not been properly raised in the courts below.

[34] Notice of Proposed Rule, 67 Fed. Reg. 31,403, 31,475-6 (May 9, 2002).

[35] Bryant v. Adventist Health Sys., 289 F.3d at 1168-1169.

[36] Notice of Final Rule, 68 Fed. Reg. 53,221, 53,243-5 (Sept. 9, 2003). Comments also expressed concerns that EMTALA would usurp existing protections for inpatients.

[37] 42 C.F.R. § 489.24(d)(2). Inpatients are still protected by other Medicare conditions of participation. Persons admitted for elective treatment or diagnosis are still covered under EMTALA. Id.

[38] 73 Fed. Reg. 48,656-61.

[39] See supra note 22 and accompanying text.

[40] 42 C.F.R. 489.24(f)(2).

[41] Moses v. Providence Hosp. & Med. Ctrs., Inc., 561 F.3d 573, 582 (6th Cir. 2009), cert. denied, Providence Hosp. v. Moses, 130 S. Ct. 3499 (June 28, 2010).

[42] Id. at 583.

[43] Id.

[44] Providence Hosp. v. Moses, 130 S. Ct. 3499 (June 28, 2010) (denying certiorari).

[45] Moses v. Providence Hosp. & Med. Ctrs., Inc., 561 F.3d at 583-584.

[46] Lilly v. Harper Hosp. Assocs., 2009 U.S. Dist. LEXIS 121405 (E.D. Mich. Dec. 3, 2009) (finding that defendant hospital did not violate EMTALA where patient was admitted for treatment and subsequently died at the hospital).

[47] 75 Fed. Reg. 80762 (Dec. 23, 2010).

[48] 75 Fed. Reg. 80765.

[49] In re Baby K, 16 F.3d 590 (4th Cir. 1994).

[50] Id. at 596-7.

[51] Id. EMTALA explicitly preempts any state laws that directly conflict with EMTALA's provisions. 42 U.S.C. § 1395dd(f). The Fourth Circuit later clarified Baby K's holding in Bryan v. Univ. of Virginia, ruling that EMTALA only mandates treating a patient's emergency medical condition, not the patient's general medical condition. Bryan v. Univ. of Virginia, 95 F.3d at 352. Therefore, had the hospital admitted Baby K after stabilizing her emergency respiratory distress, it would not have been required to then treat her underlying anencephaly beyond warmth and nutrition. Id.

[52] 42 C.F.R. § 489.24(e)(2).

[53] 42 C.F.R. § 489.24(e)(1)(ii)(B).

[54] Moses v. Providence Hosp. & Med. Ctrs., Inc., 561 F.3d at 579-582.

[55] H.Rept. 99-241, at 6.

[56] Moses, 2009 U.S. App. LEXIS 7049, at 17-19.

[57] 42 U.S.C. § 1395dd(d)(2)(A) (emphasis added).

In: Hospital Emergency Departments
Editor: Daniel T. Lee

ISBN: 978-1-63482-170-4

Chapter 3

OVERVIEW OF EMERGENCY DEPARTMENT VISITS IN THE UNITED STATES, 2011*

Audrey J. Weiss, Lauren M. Wier, Carol Stocks, and Janice Blanchard

INTRODUCTION

Emergency departments (EDs) provide a significant source of medical care in the United States, with over 131 million total ED visits occurring in 2011.[1] Over the past decade, the increase in ED utilization has outpaced growth of the general population, despite a national decline in the total number of ED facilities.[2,3] In 2009, approximately half of all hospital inpatient admissions originated in the ED.[4] In particular, EDs were the primary portal of entry for hospital admission for uninsured and publicly insured patients (privately insured patients were more likely to be directly admitted to the hospital from a doctor's office or clinic).[5]

ED utilization reflects the greater health needs of the surrounding community and may provide the only readily available care for individuals who cannot obtain care elsewhere.[6] Many ED visits are "resource sensitive" and potentially preventable, meaning that access to high-quality, community-based health care can prevent the need for a portion of ED visits.

---

* This is an edited, reformatted and augmented version of HCUP Statistical Brief, No. 174, issued by the Agency for Healthcare Research and Quality, June 2014.

This HCUP Statistical Brief presents data on ED visits in the United States in 2011. Patient and hospital characteristics for two types of ED visits are provided: ED visits with admission to the same hospital and ED visits resulting in discharge, which includes patients who were stabilized in the ED and then discharged home, transferred to another hospital, or any other disposition. The most frequent conditions treated by patient age group also are presented for both types of ED visits. All differences between estimates noted in the text are statistically significant at the .0005 level or better.

HIGHLIGHTS

- In 2011, there were about 421 visits to the emergency department (ED) for every 1,000 individuals in the population.
- More than five times as many individuals who visited an ED were discharged as were admitted to the same hospital.
- Among patients younger than 18 years, the most common reasons for admission to the hospital after an ED visit were acute bronchitis (infants younger than 1 year), asthma (patients aged 1–17 years), and pneumonia (infants and patients aged 1–17 years).
- For adults aged 45–84 years, septicemia (infection in the bloodstream) was the most frequent reason for admission to the hospital after an ED visit.
- Medicare was the primary payer for more than half of ED visits that resulted in admission to the same hospital.
- The most common reasons for ED visits resulting in discharge were fever and otitis media (infants and patients aged 1–17 years), superficial injury (all age groups except infants), open wounds of the head, neck, and trunk (patients aged 1–17 years and adults aged 85+ years), nonspecific chest pain (adults aged 45 years and older), and abdominal pain and back pain (all adult age groups except those aged 85+ years).
- Rural areas had a higher rate of ED visits resulting in discharge compared with urban areas.

Findings

Emergency department visits by selected patient and hospital characteristics, 2011

In 2011, rates of ED visits varied by the patient's sex, age group, residence, and hospital region (Figure 1).

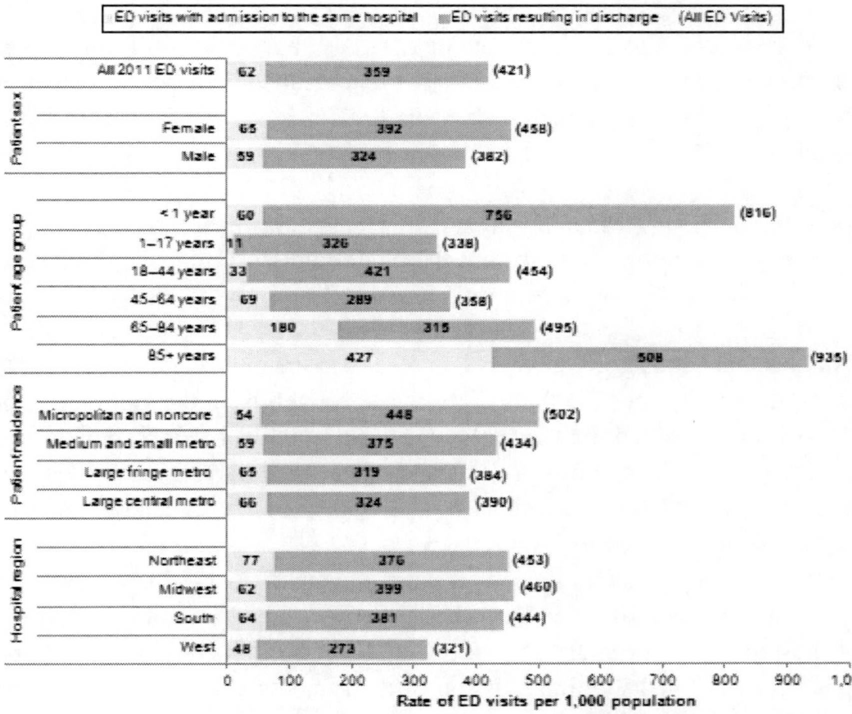

Source: Agency for Healthcare Research and Quality (AHRQ), Center for Delivery, Organization, and Markets, Healthcare Cost and Utilization Project (HCUP), Nationwide Emergency Department Sample (NEDS), 2011.

Note: "ED visits resulting in discharge" includes patients who were stabilized in the ED and then discharged home, transferred to another hospital, or any other disposition.

Figure 1. Rate of emergency department visits by the patient's sex, age group, residence, and hospital region, 2011.

- In 2011, more than five times as many individuals who visited the ED were discharged as were admitted to the same hospital.

Overall, in 2011 there were 421 ED visits per 1,000 population. More than five times as many individuals who visited the ED were discharged (359 per 1,000 population) as were admitted to the same hospital (62 per 1,000 population).

- Overall, females had about a 20 percent higher rate of ED visits than males.

Females had a higher overall rate of ED visits than males (458 versus 382 per 1,000 population). The rate of ED visits that resulted in discharge was over 20 percent higher for females than males (392 versus 324 per 1,000 population).

- Infants younger than 1 year and adults aged 85 years and older had the highest rate of ED visits, but the older adults were far more likely to be admitted to the same hospital.

Infants and adults aged 85 years and older had the highest rate of ED visits overall (816 and 935 per 1,000 population, respectively) and the highest rate of ED visits that resulted in discharge (756 and 508 per 1,000 population, respectively). Adults aged 65–84 years and adults aged 85 years and older had the highest rates of ED visits with admission to the same hospital (180 and 427 per 1,000 population, respectively).

Among infants younger than 1 year and patients aged 1–17 years and 18–44 years, fewer than 10 percent of all ED visits resulted in admission to the same hospital (7.4 percent, 3.3 percent, and 7.3 percent, respectively). The proportion of ED visits with admission to the same hospital increased as age increased among the following groups: 45–64 years (19.3 percent), 65–84 years (36.4 percent), and 85 years and older (45.7 percent).

- Rural areas had the highest rate of ED visits resulting in discharge.

Rural areas (micropolitan and noncore areas) had the highest rate of ED visits that resulted in discharge in 2011 (448 per 1,000 population) compared with urban areas: medium and small metropolitan areas (375), large metropolitan counties (319), and large metropolitan cities (324). ED visits with admission to the same hospital did not differ substantially by patient residence.

- Western States had the lowest rate of ED visits.

Western States had the lowest rate of ED visits overall (321 per 1,000 population) compared with the other three U.S. regions: South (444), Midwest (460), and Northeast (453). The lower ED visit rate in the West occurred for ED visits with admission to the same hospital (48 per 1,000 population) and ED visits resulting in discharge (273 per 1,000 population).

The proportions of ED visits that were attributable to each expected primary payer are provided in Figure 2.

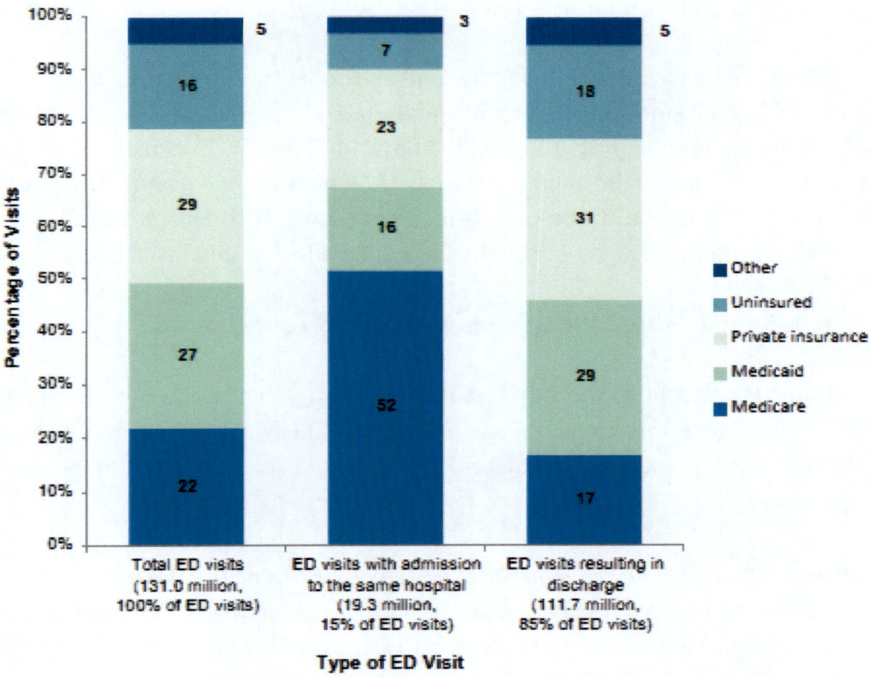

Source: Agency for Healthcare Research and Quality (AHRQ), Center for Delivery, Organization, and Markets, Healthcare Cost and Utilization Project (HCUP), Nationwide Emergency Department Sample (NEDS), 2011.

Note: "ED visits resulting in discharge" includes patients who were stabilized in the ED and then discharged home, transferred to another hospital, or any other disposition.

Figure 2. Proportions of emergency department visits by expected primary payer, 2011.

- Among all ED visits in 2011, private insurance and Medicaid were the most common expected primary payers.

Of the 131 million total ED visits in 2011, 29 percent were billed to private insurance, 27 percent to Medicaid, and 22 percent to Medicare. For 16 percent of all ED visits, there was no insurance coverage.

- For ED visits with admission to the same hospital, Medicare was the most common primary payer.

Medicare was billed for 52 percent of the 19.3 million ED visits that resulted in admission to the same hospital in 2011. Private insurance was the second most common primary expected payer, billing for 23 percent of all ED visits that resulted in hospital admission, followed by Medicaid, which was billed for 16 percent of these ED visits. Approximately 7 percent of ED visits with admission to the same hospital were not covered by any insurance.

- For ED visits resulting in discharge, nearly one-fifth were uninsured.

Fully 18 percent of the 111.7 million ED visits that resulted in discharge had no insurance coverage. Private insurance and Medicaid were the most common primary payers for these ED visits (31 percent and 29 percent, respectively).

Reasons for Emergency Department Visits by Patient Age Group, 2011

Tables 1 and 2 provide the most common principal conditions identified in 2011 for admission to the same hospital after an ED visit (Table 1) and ED visits resulting in discharge (Table 2) by patient age group.

- The five most common reasons for admission to the same hospital after an ED visit constituted between 18.2 percent and 40.8 percent of the ED visits, depending on the patient's age group.

Table 1. Top five principal conditions for admission to the same hospital after an emergency department visit, by age group, 2011

Principal condition[a]	Number and rank[b] of ED visits with admission to the same hospital, by age group											
	<1 year		1–17 years		18–44 years		45–64 years		65–84 years		85+ years	
	n	Rank	n	Rank	n	Rank	n	Rank	n	Rank	n	Rank
Total ED visits with admission to the same hospital	238,317		799,637		3,734,009		5,679,839		6,421,521		2,449,425	
Acute bronchitis	52,200	1										
Pneumonia (except that caused by tuberculosis and sexually transmitted diseases)	17,600	2	69,400	2			203,500	3	328,000	3	149,400	3
Urinary tract infections	11,900	3									125,400	4
Fever of unknown origin	7,900	4										
Hemolytic jaundice and perinatal jaundice	7,700	5										
Asthma			76,900	1								
Appendicitis and other appendiceal conditions			59,200	3								
Mood disorders			37,400	4	226,300	1						
Skin and subcutaneous tissue infections			33,300	5	133,700	3	161,800	5				
Diabetes mellitus with complications					134,200	2						
Schizophrenia and other psychotic disorders					120,400	4						

Table 1. (Continued)

Principal condition[a]	Number and rank[b] of ED visits with admission to the same hospital, by age group											
	<1 year		1–17 years		18–44 years		45–64 years		65–84 years		85+ years	
	n	Rank	n	Rank	n	Rank	n	Rank	n	Rank	n	Rank
Biliary tract disease					116,300	5						
Septicemia (except in labor)							237,500	1	392,700	1	167,500	2
Nonspecific chest pain							233,200	2				
Chronic obstructive pulmonary disease and bronchiectasis							198,500	4	309,000	4		
Congestive heart failure, nonhypertensive									350,100	2	190,500	1
Cardiac dysrhythmias									278,600	5		
Fracture of neck of femur (hip)											105,600	5

Source: Agency for Healthcare Research and Quality (AHRQ), Center for Delivery, Organization, and Markets, Healthcare Cost and Utilization Project (HCUP), Nationwide Emergency Department Sample (NIS), 2011.

[a] Principal conditions are based on the first-listed diagnosis on the hospital discharge record and are classified using AHRQ's Clinical Classifications Software (CCS). Two general CCS "other" conditions are not reported in the table for infants aged <1 year: other perinatal conditions (26,200 ED visits) and other upper respiratory infections (8,200 ED visits). "Other" CCS categories include miscellaneous, otherwise unclassifiable diagnoses that may be difficult to interpret as a group.

[b] Rank of the principal condition by number of ED visits within each age group

Table 2. Top five principal conditions for emergency department visits resulting in discharge, by age group, 2011

Principal condition[a]	Number and rank[b] of ED visits resulting in discharge, by age group											
	<1 year		1–17 years		18–44 years		45–64 years		65–84 years		85+ years	
	n	Rank	n	Rank	n	Rank	n	Rank	n	Rank	n	Rank
Total ED visits resulting in discharge[c]	3,021,782		22,819,322		47,788,338		23,953,917		11,220,150		2,915,116	
Fever of unknown origin	269,900	1	842,400	5								
Otitis media and related conditions	266,200	2	1,266,500	2								
Acute bronchitis	181,000	3										
Viral infections	145,600	4										
Nausea and vomiting	121,300	5										
Superficial injury, contusion			1,575,900	1	2,178,700	3	1,066,500	5	565,800	2	213,400	1
Open wounds of head, neck, and trunk			1,142,600	3							96,200	4
Sprains and strains			1,061,100	4	3,181,700	1	1,350,800	2				
Abdominal pain					2,958,300	2	1,197,600	4	425,200	3		
Spondylosis, intervertebral disc disorders, other back problems					1,827,600	4	1,200,600	3	368,000	4		
Headache, including migraine					1,770,000	5						
Nonspecific chest pain							1,525,200	1	643,000	1	117,200	3

Table 2. (Continued)

Principal condition[a]	Number and rank[b] of ED visits resulting in discharge, by age group											
	<1 year		1–17 years		18–44 years		45–64 years		65–84 years		85+ years	
	n	Rank	n	Rank	n	Rank	n	Rank	n	Rank	n	Rank
Urinary tract infections									359,900	5	127,100	2
Open wounds of extremities											82,800	5

Source: Agency for Healthcare Research and Quality (AHRQ), Center for Delivery, Organization, and Markets, Healthcare Cost and Utilization Project (HCUP), Nationwide Emergency Department Sample (NIS), 2011.

[a] Principal conditions are based on the first-listed diagnosis on the ED visit record and are classified using AHRQ's Clinical Classifications Software (CCS). General CCS "other" conditions are not reported in the table and include the following conditions by age group: other upper respiratory infections (<1 year: 540,700 ED visits; 1–17 years: 2,550,600 ED visits; 18–44: 1,926,500 ED visits); other perinatal conditions (<1 year: 151,400 ED visits); other injuries and conditions due to external causes (1–17 years: 1,075,500 ED visits; 85+ years: 126,200 ED visits). "Other" CCS categories include miscellaneous, otherwise unclassifiable diagnoses that may be difficult to interpret as a group.

[b] Rank of the principal condition by number of ED visits within each age group

[c] "ED visits resulting in discharge" include patients who were stabilized in the ED and then discharged home, transferred to another hospital, or any other disposition.

In 2011, the five most common principal conditions accounted for 40.8 percent of all infant admissions to the same hospital after an ED visit. The five top-ranked reasons constituted about one-third of the admissions after an ED visit among patients aged 1–17 years (34.5 percent) and adults aged 85 years and older (30.1 percent). The most frequent principal conditions accounted for one-fourth or less of the admissions after an ED visit among adults aged 18–44 years (19.6 percent), 45–64 years (18.2 percent), and 65–84 years (25.8 percent).

- Pneumonia and other respiratory conditions were top-ranked reasons for admission to the same hospital after an ED visit for all age groups except those aged 18–44 years.

In 2011, pneumonia was either the second or third most common reason for admission to the same hospital after an ED visit for all age groups except adults aged 18–44 years (pneumonia was the ninth most common condition in this age group, data not shown).

Other respiratory conditions also were common for most age groups. Acute bronchitis was the most common reason for admission to the same hospital after an ED visit for infants, and asthma was the most common diagnosis for patients aged 1–17 years. Chronic obstructive pulmonary disease and bronchiectasis was the fourth most common reason for admission to the same hospital after an ED visit for adults aged 45–64 years and 65–84 years.

- Septicemia and cardiac conditions were top reasons for admission to the same hospital after an ED visit among adults aged 45 years and older.

Septicemia was the most common reason for admission to the same hospital after an ED visit among adults aged 45–64 years and 65–84 years. Septicemia also was the second most common diagnosis among adults aged 85 years and older.

Congestive heart failure was the top-ranked reason for admission to the same hospital after an ED visit among adults aged 85 years and older and the second most common reason among adults aged 65–84 years. Other cardiac conditions also were common: nonspecific chest pain was the second most common reason for admission to the same hospital after an ED visit among adults aged 45–64 years, and cardiac dysrhythmias were the fifth most common reason among those aged 65–84 years.

- Mood disorders were a common type of diagnosis among younger patients admitted to the same hospital after an ED visit.

A mood disorders diagnosis was the most common reason for admission to the same hospital after an ED visit among adults aged 18–44 years. Schizophrenia and other psychotic disorders also were common among this age group, ranking fourth among reasons for admission to the same hospital. Mood disorders were the fourth most common type of diagnosis among patients aged 1–17 years.

- The five most common reasons for ED visits resulting in discharge constituted between 21.1 percent and 32.6 percent of the ED visits, depending on the patient's age group.

In 2011, the five top-ranked principal conditions accounted for 32.6 percent of all ED visits for infants that resulted in discharge. The five most common reasons constituted about one-fourth of ED visits among patients aged 1–17 years (25.8 percent), adults aged 18–44 years (24.9 percent), and adults aged 45–64 years (26.5 percent). The most frequent principal conditions accounted for about one-fifth of ED visits that resulted in discharge among adults aged 65–84 years (21.1 percent) and adults aged 85 years and older (21.8 percent).

- Fever and otitis media were common principal conditions diagnosed during ED visits resulting in discharge among patients younger than 18 years.

Fever of unknown origin was the most common diagnosis for ED visits that resulted in discharge among infants younger than 1 year. Fever also was the fifth most common condition among patients aged 1–17 years. Otitis media and related conditions (ear infections) was the second most frequent reason for ED visits resulting in discharge among infants and patients aged 1–17 years.

- Injuries—including contusions, open wounds, and sprains—were common reasons for ED visits resulting in discharge among all age groups except infants.

Superficial injury was the most common reason for ED visits resulting in discharge among patients aged 1–17 years and adults aged 85 years and older.

Superficial injury also was among the top five reasons for ED visits resulting in discharge among other adult age groups, ranking second among adults aged 65–84 years, third among adults aged 18–44 years, and fifth among adults aged 45–64 years.

Other injury-related conditions also were commonly observed during ED visits resulting in discharge. Open wounds of the head, neck, and trunk were frequent reasons for ED visits that resulted in discharge among patients aged 1–17 years and adults aged 85 years and older. Sprains and strains were common among patients aged 1–17 years, adults aged 18–44 years (where it was the top-ranked condition), and adults aged 45–64 years. Open wounds of extremities were the fifth most common type of diagnosis among adults aged 85 years and older.

- Nonspecific chest pain was a top-ranked principal condition for ED visits resulting in discharge among adults aged 45 years and older.

Nonspecific chest pain was the most common reason for ED visits that resulted in discharge for adults aged 45–64 years and 65–84 years. Nonspecific chest pain was the third most common diagnosis among adults aged 85 years and older.

- Abdominal pain and back problems were among the five most frequent reasons for ED visits resulting in discharge among all adult age groups except those aged 85 years and older.

Abdominal pain was one of the most common reasons for adult ED visits that resulted in discharge, ranking as the second most common reason among adults aged 18–44 years, ranking fourth among adults aged 45–64 years, and ranking third among adults aged 65–84 years.

Spondylosis, intervertebral disc disorders, and other back problems also were a common type of diagnosis for adult ED visits resulting in discharge, ranking fourth among adults aged 18–44 years and 65–84 years and ranking third among adults aged 45–64 years.

Data Source

The estimates in this Statistical Brief are based upon data from the Healthcare Cost and Utilization Project (HCUP) Nationwide Emergency

Department Sample (NEDS), 2011. The statistics were generated from HCUPnet, a free, online query system that provides users with *immediate access* to the largest set of publicly available, all-payer national, regional, and State-level hospital care databases from HCUP.[7]

Many statistical tests were conducted for this Statistical Brief. Thus, to decrease the number of false-positive results, we reduced the significance level to .0005 for individual tests.

Definitions

Diagnoses, ICD-9-CM, and Clinical Classifications Software (CCS)

The principal diagnosis is that condition established after study to be chiefly responsible for the patient's admission to the hospital. Secondary diagnoses are concomitant conditions that coexist at the time of admission or develop during the stay.

ICD-9-CM is the International Classification of Diseases, Ninth Revision, Clinical Modification, which assigns numeric codes to diagnoses. There are approximately 14,000 ICD-9-CM diagnosis codes.

CCS categorizes ICD-9-CM diagnoses into a manageable number of clinically meaningful categories.[8] This "clinical grouper" makes it easier to quickly understand patterns of diagnoses. CCS categories identified as "Other" typically are not reported; these categories include miscellaneous, otherwise unclassifiable diagnoses that may be difficult to interpret as a group.

Types of Hospitals Included in HCUP

HCUP is based on data from community hospitals, which are defined as short-term, non-Federal, general, and other hospitals, excluding hospital units of other institutions (e.g., prisons). HCUP data include obstetrics and gynecology, otolaryngology, orthopedic, cancer, pediatric, public, and academic medical hospitals. Excluded are long-term care, rehabilitation, psychiatric, and alcoholism and chemical dependency hospitals. Community hospitals included in the Nationwide Emergency Department Sample (NEDS) have hospital-based emergency departments and no more than 90 percent of their ED visits resulting in admission.

Unit of Analysis

The unit of analysis is the emergency department (ED) encounter, not a person or patient. This means that a person who is seen in the ED multiple times in one year will be counted each time as a separate "encounter" in the ED.

Location of Patients' Residence

Place of residence is based on the urban-rural classification scheme for U.S. counties developed by the National Center for Health Statistics (NCHS). For this Statistical Brief, we collapsed the NCHS categories into either urban or rural according to the following:

Urban

- Large Central Metropolitan: includes metropolitan areas with 1 million or more residents
- Large Fringe Metropolitan: includes counties of metropolitan areas with 1 million or more residents
- Medium and Small Metropolitan: includes areas with 50,000 to 999,999 residents.

Rural

- Micropolitan and Noncore: includes nonmetropolitan counties (i.e., counties with no town greater than 50,000 residents).

Payer

Payer is the expected primary payer for the hospital stay. To make coding uniform across all HCUP data sources, payer combines detailed categories into general groups:

- Medicare: includes patients covered by fee-for-service and managed care Medicare
- Medicaid: includes patients covered by fee-for-service and managed care Medicaid
- Private Insurance: includes Blue Cross, commercial carriers, and private health maintenance organizations (HMOs) and preferred provider organizations (PPOs)
- Uninsured: includes an insurance status of "self-pay" and "no charge"
- Other: includes Worker's Compensation, TRICARE/CHAMPUS, CHAMPVA, Title V, and other government programs.

Hospital stays billed to the State Children's Health Insurance Program (SCHIP) may be classified as Medicaid, Private Insurance, or Other, depending on the structure of the State program. Because most State data do not identify SCHIP patients specifically, it is not possible to present this information separately.

When more than one payer is listed for a hospital discharge, the first-listed payer is used.

Region

Region is one of the four regions defined by the U.S. Census Bureau:

- Northeast: Maine, New Hampshire, Vermont, Massachusetts, Rhode Island, Connecticut, New York, New Jersey, and Pennsylvania
- Midwest: Ohio, Indiana, Illinois, Michigan, Wisconsin, Minnesota, Iowa, Missouri, North Dakota, South Dakota, Nebraska, and Kansas
- South: Delaware, Maryland, District of Columbia, Virginia, West Virginia, North Carolina, South Carolina, Georgia, Florida, Kentucky, Tennessee, Alabama, Mississippi, Arkansas, Louisiana, Oklahoma, and Texas
- West: Montana, Idaho, Wyoming, Colorado, New Mexico, Arizona, Utah, Nevada, Washington, Oregon, California, Alaska, and Hawaii

About HCUP

The Healthcare Cost and Utilization Project (HCUP, pronounced "H-Cup") is a family of health care databases and related software tools and products developed through a Federal-State-Industry partnership and sponsored by the Agency for Healthcare Research and Quality (AHRQ). HCUP databases bring together the data collection efforts of State data organizations, hospital associations, private data organizations, and the Federal government to create a national information resource of encounter-level health care data (HCUP Partners). HCUP includes the largest collection of longitudinal hospital care data in the United States, with all-payer, encounter-level information beginning in 1988. These databases enable research on a broad range of health policy issues, including cost and quality of health services, medical practice patterns, access to health care programs, and outcomes of treatments at the national, State, and local market levels.

HCUP would not be possible without the contributions of the following data collection Partners from across the United States:

Alaska State Hospital and Nursing Home Association
Arizona Department of Health Services
Arkansas Department of Health
California Office of Statewide Health Planning and Development
Colorado Hospital Association
Connecticut Hospital Association
Florida Agency for Health Care Administration
Georgia Hospital Association
Hawaii Health Information Corporation
Illinois Department of Public Health
Indiana Hospital Association
Iowa Hospital Association
Kansas Hospital Association
Kentucky Cabinet for Health and Family Services
Louisiana Department of Health and Hospitals
Maine Health Data Organization
Maryland Health Services Cost Review Commission
Massachusetts Center for Health Information and Analysis
Michigan Health & Hospital Association
Minnesota Hospital Association
Mississippi Department of Health
Missouri Hospital Industry Data Institute
Montana MHA - An Association of Montana Health Care Providers
Nebraska Hospital Association
Nevada Department of Health and Human Services
New Hampshire Department of Health & Human Services
New Jersey Department of Health
New Mexico Department of Health
New York State Department of Health
North Carolina Department of Health and Human Services
North Dakota (data provided by the Minnesota Hospital Association)
Ohio Hospital Association
Oklahoma State Department of Health
Oregon Association of Hospitals and Health Systems
Oregon Health Policy and Research
Pennsylvania Health Care Cost Containment Council

Rhode Island Department of Health
South Carolina Budget & Control Board
South Dakota Association of Healthcare Organizations
Tennessee Hospital Association
Texas Department of State Health Services
Utah Department of Health
Vermont Association of Hospitals and Health Systems
Virginia Health Information
Washington State Department of Health
West Virginia Health Care Authority
Wisconsin Department of Health Services
Wyoming Hospital Association

About Statistical Briefs

HCUP Statistical Briefs are descriptive summary reports presenting statistics on hospital inpatient and emergency department use and costs, quality of care, access to care, medical conditions, procedures, patient populations, and other topics. The reports use HCUP administrative health care data.

About the NEDS

The HCUP Nationwide Emergency Department Database (NEDS) is a unique and powerful database that yields national estimates of emergency department (ED) visits. The NEDS was constructed using records from both the HCUP State Emergency Department Databases (SEDD) and the State Inpatient Databases (SID). The SEDD capture information on ED visits that do not result in an admission (i.e., treat-and-release visits and transfers to another hospital); the SID contains information on patients initially seen in the emergency room and then admitted to the same hospital. The NEDS was created to enable analyses of ED utilization patterns and support public health professionals, administrators, policymakers, and clinicians in their decisionmaking regarding this critical source of care. The NEDS is produced annually beginning in 2006.

About HCUPnet

HCUPnet is an online query system that offers instant access to the largest set of all-payer health care databases that are publicly available. HCUPnet has an easy step-by-step query system that creates tables and graphs of national and regional statistics as well as data trends for community hospitals in the United States. HCUPnet generates statistics using data from HCUP's Nationwide Inpatient Sample (NIS), the Kids' Inpatient Database (KID), the Nationwide Emergency Department Sample (NEDS), the State Inpatient Databases (SID), and the State Emergency Department Databases (SEDD).

For More Information

For more information about HCUP, visit http://www.hcup-us.ahrq.gov/.

End Notes

[1] HCUPnet. 2011 National Statistics, All ED Visits. http://hcupnet.ahrq.gov/HCUPnet.jsp. Accessed May 7, 2014.

[2] Tang N, Stein J, Hsia RY, Maselli JH, Gonzales R. Trends and characteristics of US emergency department visits, 1997–2007. Journal of the American Medical Association. 2010;304(6):664–70.

[3] Goodell S, DeLia D, Cantor JC. Emergency Department Utilization and Capacity. 2009, Robert Wood Johnson Foundation Policy Brief No. 17. Princeton, NJ: Robert Wood Johnson Foundation. http://www.rwjf.org/content/dam/farm/reports/issue briefs/2009/rwjf43566. Accessed May 7, 2014.

[4] Morganti-Gonzalez K, Baufman S, Blanchard J, Abir M, Iyer N, Smith A, et al. The Evolving Role of Emergency Departments in the United States. RAND RR 280-ACEP. Santa Monica, CA: Rand Corp; May 2013.

[5] Ibid. Note: excludes live births.

[6] Tang et al., 2010.

[7] Agency for Healthcare Research and Quality. HCUPnet web site. http://hcupnet.ahrq.gov/. Accessed May 7, 2014.

[8] HCUP Clinical Classifications Software (CCS). Healthcare Cost and Utilization Project (HCUP). U.S. Agency for Healthcare Research and Quality, Rockville, MD. Updated April 2014.http://www.hcup-us.ahrq.gov/toolssoftware/ccs/ccs.jsp. Accessed May 7, 2014.

In: Hospital Emergency Departments
Editor: Daniel T. Lee
ISBN: 978-1-63482-170-4

Chapter 4

TRENDS IN EMERGENCY DEPARTMENT VISITS, 2006–2011*

Halcyon G. Skinner, Janice Blanchard and Anne Elixhauser

INTRODUCTION

There has been an overall increase in emergency department (ED) visits over the past two decades.[1] However, ED visits for specific conditions have shown varying patterns, and visits for some conditions have decreased in recent years.[2]

There are a number of factors that may affect both positive and negative trends in growth for condition-specific ED visits. Some of those factors are personal, such as an individual's specific health condition. Other factors are related to the community where the individual lives—for example, the availability of health care options.

Changes in health care are reflected in ED use. For example, with improved care coordination some conditions may now be more effectively managed in the outpatient setting, which reduces the need for the acute care provided by EDs.[3,4] Updated information about trends in ED use over time

* This is an edited, reformatted and augmented version of HCUP Statistical Brief, No. 179, issued by the Agency for Healthcare Research and Quality, September 2014.

reveals the changing needs of individuals in the community and emerging transformations in health care policies.

This HCUP Statistical Brief presents data on changes in overall ED visits from 2006 through 2011. ED visit rates are reported by patient demographic characteristics and tracked by patient age. Changes in ED visit rates for the most common conditions and the conditions with the greatest changes also are provided. Changes in rates are considered statistically significant if the p-value is 0.05 or less.

HIGHLIGHTS

- The rate of ED visits over the 5- year period from 2006 to 2011 increased among patients aged 45–64 years (8 percent increase).
- Across all conditions with at least 100,000 ED visits in 2006, the most rapid increase (74 percent) by 2011 occurred for septicemia, a bloodstream infection. The most rapid decrease (30 percent) occurred for noninfectious gastroenteritis.
- Between 2006 and 2011, the rate of ED visits for substance-related disorders (not including alcohol) increased 48 percent. Over the same time period, ED visits for alcohol-related disorders increased 34 percent.
- Among the most common reasons for ED visits, *sprains and strains* and *superficial injury* each experienced approximately a 10 percent decrease in the rate of ED visits from 2006 to 2011.
- Increases in the rates of ED visits were observed for abdominal pain (18 percent) and nonspecific chest pain (13 percent).

Findings

Changes in ED Visits Rates between 2006 and 2011

Table 1 presents ED visit rates in 2006 and 2011 by patient characteristics, along with the percent change over that time period.

- The rate of emergency department visits increased for individuals aged 45–64 years.

The rate of ED visits for individuals aged 45–64 years increased from 33,000 per 100,000 population in 2006 to 35,800 per 100,000 population in 2011. This was an 8 percent increase over the 5-year time period.

Table 1. Changes in ED visit rates (per 100,000 population) by patient characteristics, 2006 and 2011

Characteristic	Rate per 100,000 population		Percent change
	2006	2011	
Total rate for all ED visits	40,200	42,100	4.5
Age group, years			
<1	88,900	81,600	–8.3
1–17	32,700	33,800	3.1
18–44	43,300	45,400	5.0
45–64	33,000	35,800	8.3
65–84	48,900	49,500	1.3
85+	90,900	93,500	2.8
Sex			
Male	37,300	38,200	2.4
Female	43,000	45,800	6.3
Median income for ZIP Code			
Low	49,400	51,900	5.3
Not low	36,100	37,700	4.5
Patient residence			
Large central metro	31,900	39,000	22.3
Large fringe metro (suburbs)	40,600	38,400	–5.5
Medium and small metro	43,600	43,400	–0.5
Micropolitan and noncore (rural)	47,300	50,200	6.2
Region			
Northeast	43,200	45,300	4.8
Midwest	42,200	46,000	9.2
South	43,000	44,400	3.3
West	31,600	32,100	1.6

Source: Agency for Healthcare Research and Quality (AHRQ), Center for Delivery, Organization, and Markets, Healthcare Cost and Utilization Project (HCUP), Nationwide Emergency Department Sample (NIS), 2006 and 2011.

All rates were rounded to the nearest 100. Percent change is reported based on nonrounded rates.

- The rate of emergency department visits increased for women.

The rate of ED visits increased from 43,000 per 100,000 women in 2006 to 45,800 per 100,000 women in 2011, which represented a 6 percent increase over 5 years.

- Large central cities had the largest increase in the rate of ED visits.

Between 2006 and 2011, large central metropolitan areas experienced a 22 percent increase in the rate of ED visits over 5 years, from 31,900 to 39,000 visits per 100,000 population.

Changes in ED Visits Rates by Patient Age, 2006–2011

Figure 1 presents the trend in ED visit rates (per 100,000 population) by patient age group from 2006 through 2011.

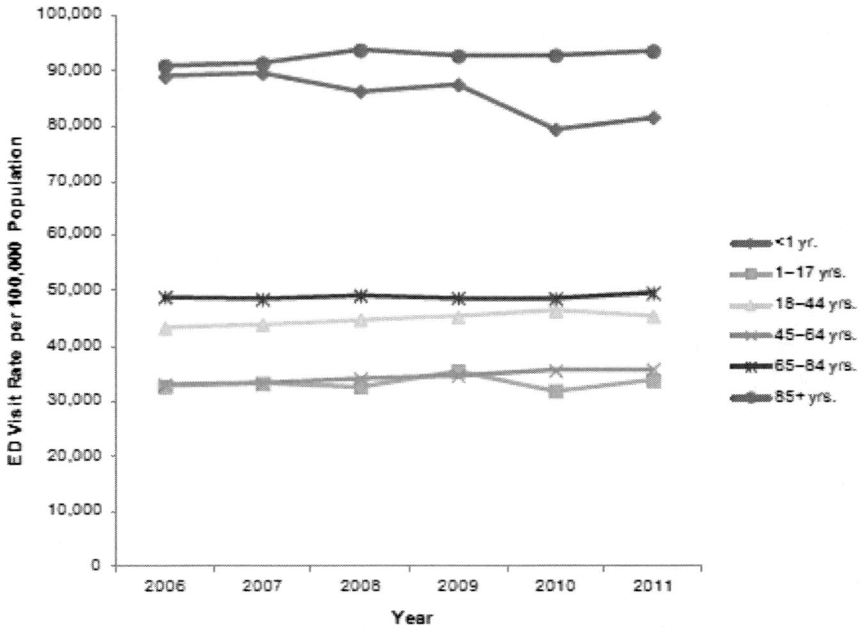

Source: Agency for Healthcare Research and Quality (AHRQ), Center for Delivery, Organization, and Markets, Healthcare Cost and Utilization Project (HCUP), Nationwide Emergency Department Sample (NEDS), 2006–2011.

Figure 1. Trends in ED visit rates by patient age, 2006–2011.

- The ED visit rate was consistently highest among the oldest patients.

The rate of ED visits was consistently highest among the individuals aged 85 years and older, with rates essentially unchanged between 2006 and 2011.

- The rate of ED visits declined among infants.

In 2006, the rate of ED visits for infants younger than 1 year was approximately as high as the rate for adults aged 85 years and older (89,000 visits per 100,000 population for infants versus 90,900 per 100,000 population for adults aged 85 years and older). However, the ED visit rate for infants declined by 11 percent for the 5-year period from 2006 to 2011. By 2011, the ED visit rate for infants was significantly lower than the rate for adults aged 85 years and older (81,600 versus 93,500 per 100,000 population).

- The rate of ED visits increased gradually for individuals aged 45–64 years.

The rate of ED visits increased consistently between 1 and 3 percent per year for individuals aged 45–64 years from 2006 to 2011. The net change over the 5-year period was an 8 percent increase for individuals in this age group.

Most Frequent Conditions Seen in the ED and Changes in ED Visits Rates, 2006 Through 2011

Figure 2 presents the conditions that were most commonly seen in the ED in 2006 and examines the changes in ED visit rates for those conditions in 2011.

- The rates of ED visits decreased for the two most common minor trauma conditions.

The rate of ED visits for the two most common conditions (sprains and strains; superficial injury and contusion) decreased substantially between 2006 and 2011. In 2006, there were about 6.4 million ED visits for sprains and strains (a rate of 2,133 visits per 100,000 population). In 2011, the rate of visits for sprains and strains declined by 9 percent to 1,933 per 100,000 population, based on over 6.0 million ED visits for this condition. Similarly, the rate of ED visits for superficial injury and contusion declined 11 percent from 2006 to 2011. In 2006 there were 6.1 million visits for superficial injury and contusion, compared with 5.7 million visits in 2011 (2,056 versus 1,832 visits per 100,000 population, respectively).

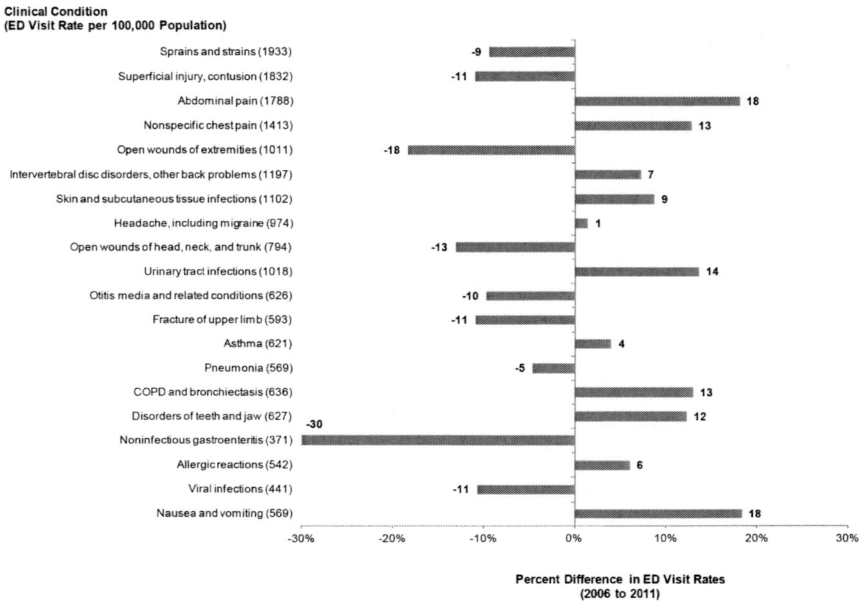

Source: Agency for Healthcare Research and Quality (AHRQ), Center for Delivery, Organization, and Markets, Healthcare Cost and Utilization Project (HCUP), Nationwide Emergency Department Sample (NEDS), 2006 and 2011.

Note: Conditions were identified using AHRQ's Clinical Classifications Software (CCS) based on first-listed diagnosis. The 20 most common conditions were those identified in 2006. Only conditions with at least 100,000 ED visits in 2006 were included. The most common conditions in 2011 are listed first. Rates are for 2011 and rounded to the nearest whole number. Percent differences were computed based on nonrounded rates. All differences were statistically significant at $p<0.05$.

Figure 2. Changes in ED visit rates from 2006 to 2011 for the 20 most common conditions seen in the ED in 2006 and the ED visit rates (per 100,000 population) in 2011.

- The rates of ED visits increased for some common nonspecific conditions.

The rates of ED visits for abdominal pain and nonspecific chest pain—the third and fourth most common reasons for ED visits overall—increased substantially between 2006 and 2011. Nonspecific diagnoses suggest that no underlying cause was found for these symptoms during the ED visit.

The rate of ED visits for abdominal pain increased by 18 percent, from 1,513 per 100,000 population in 2006 to 1,788 per 100,000 population in 2011, with 5.6 million visits in 2011. ED visits for nonspecific chest pain increased 13 percent, with rates of 1,252 visits per 100,000 population in 2006 and 1,413 visits per 100,000 population in 2011 (4.4 million visits in 2011). ED visits for nausea and vomiting increased by 18 percent.

Conditions with the Most Rapidly Increasing ED Visit Rates, 2006–2011

Figure 3 presents the conditions that had the largest increase in the rates of ED visits from 2006 to 2011 among those conditions with at least 100,000 ED visits in 2006.

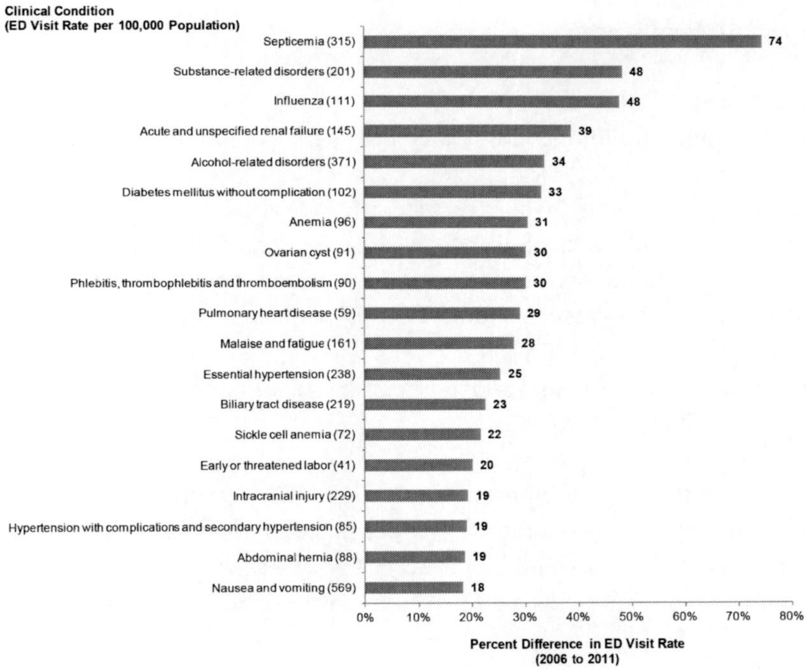

Source: Agency for Healthcare Research and Quality (AHRQ), Center for Delivery, Organization, and Markets, Healthcare Cost and Utilization Project (HCUP), Nationwide Emergency Department Sample (NEDS), 2006 and 2011.

Note: Conditions were identified using AHRQ's Clinical Classifications Software (CCS) based on first-listed diagnosis. Only conditions with at least 100,000 ED visits in 2006 were included. The most common conditions in 2011 are listed first. Rates are for 2011 and rounded to the nearest whole number. Percent differences are computed based on nonrounded rates. All differences were statistically significant at $p<0.05$.

Figure 3. Conditions with the largest increases in ED visit rates from 2006 to 2011 and the ED visit rates (per 100,000 population) in 2011.

- ED visits for two infection-related diagnoses increased substantially between 2006 and 2011.

The rate of ED visits for septicemia increased 74 percent from 2006 to 2011. There were about 538,000 ED visits for septicemia in 2006 (180 visits per 100,000 population) and 980,000 ED visits in 2011 (315 visits per 100,000 population). The rate of ED visits for influenza increased by 48 percent during this time period, from 75 visits per 100,000 population in 2006 to 111 visits per 100,000 population in 2011. (Influenza infection rates are known to vary considerably from year to year.[5])

- Visits to the ED for substance-related disorders (not including alcohol) and for alcohol-related disorders increased.

Between 2006 and 2011, the rate of ED visits for substance-related disorders not including alcohol increased 48 percent (from 136 to 201 visits per 100,000 population). Over the same time period, visits for alcohol-related disorders increased 34 percent from 277 to 371 visits per 100,000 population.

- ED visits for acute and unspecified renal failure increased by 39 percent from 2006 to 2011.

In 2006, there were approximately 313,000 ED visits for acute and unspecified renal failure—a rate of 105 per 100,000 population. In 2011, there were 453,000 visits for this diagnostic category—a rate of 145 per 100,000 population, which represents a 39 percent increase from 2006.

- ED visits for several common chronic conditions increased significantly from 2006 to 2011.

Diabetes mellitus visits increased 33 percent, pulmonary heart disease visits increased 29 percent, and visits for essential hypertension increased 25 percent.

- The only injury that appeared on the top 20 list of rapidly increasing conditions from 2006 to 2011 was intracranial injury.

Intracranial injury visit rates increased 19 percent, from 192 per 100,000 population in 2006 to 229 per 100,000 population in 2011.

Conditions with the Most Rapidly Decreasing ED Visit Rates, 2006–2011

Figure 4 presents the conditions with at least 100,000 ED visits in 2006 with the largest decreases in ED visit rates from 2006 to 2011.

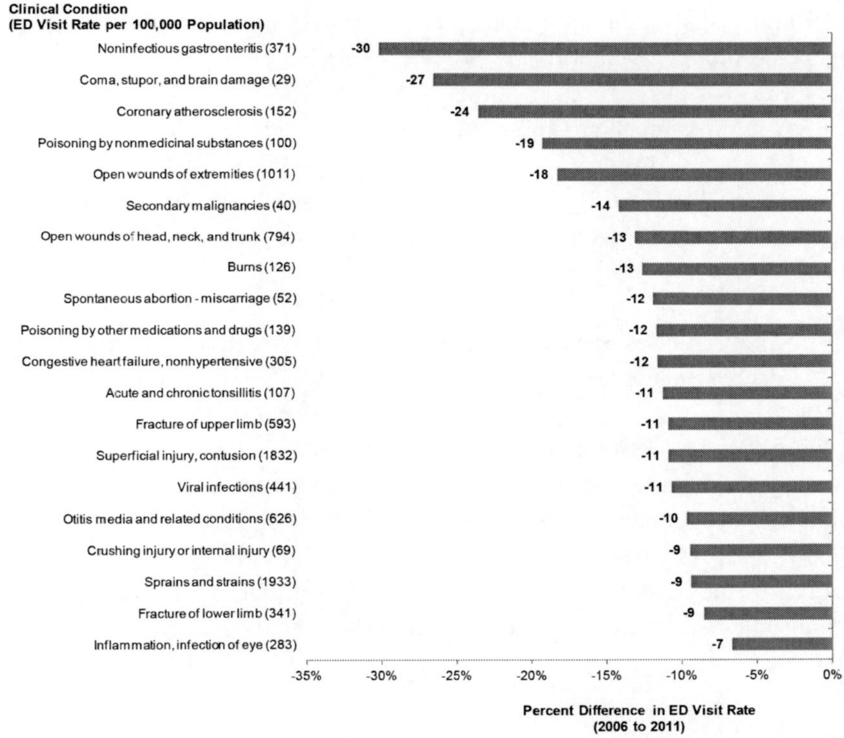

Source: Agency for Healthcare Research and Quality (AHRQ), Center for Delivery, Organization, and Markets, Healthcare Cost and Utilization Project (HCUP), Nationwide Emergency Department Sample (NEDS), 2006 and 2011.

Note: Conditions were identified using AHRQ's Clinical Classifications Software (CCS). Only first-listed diagnoses were included. Only conditions with at least 100,000 ED visits in 2011 were included. Rates are for 2011 and rounded to the nearest whole number. Percent differences were computed based on nonrounded rates. All differences were statistically significant at $p<0.05$.

Figure 4. Conditions with the largest decreases in ED visit rates from 2006 to 2011 and the ED visit rates (per 100,000 population) in 2011.

- ED visits for noninfectious gastroenteritis decreased from 2006 to 2011.

Noninfectious gastroenteritis had the largest decrease in the rate of ED visits from 2006 to 2011—a 30 percent decline over the 5-year period. In 2006, there were about 1.6 million visits for noninfectious gastroenteritis, representing a rate of 531 visits per 100,000 population. In 2011, there were 1.2 million visits for noninfectious gastroenteritis, representing a rate of 371 visits per 100,000 population.

- ED visits related to coma, stupor, and brain damage decreased.

Between 2006 and 2011, ED visits for coma, stupor, and brain damage decreased 27 percent, from a rate of 40 to 29 visits per 100,000 population, respectively.

- Many injuries appear on the top 20 list of conditions with the greatest decreases in rates.

Injuries with significant declines in the rate of ED visits included poisoning by nonmedicinal substances (19 percent); open wounds of the extremities (18 percent); open wounds of the head, neck, and trunk (13 percent); burns (13 percent); poisoning by medicines and drugs (12 percent); fracture of the upper limb (11 percent); superficial injury (11 percent); crushing injury (9 percent); sprain or strain (9 percent); and fracture of lower limb (9 percent).

- ED visits related to coronary atherosclerosis decreased.

ED visits for coronary atherosclerosis decreased 24 percent from 2006 to 2011. In 2006, there were 594,300 ED visits for coronary atherosclerosis, representing a rate of 199 visits per 100,000 population. The rate declined to 152 visits per 100,000 population in 2011, based on 474,400 visits for this condition.

- A number of infections appear on the top 20 list of conditions with the greatest decreases in rates.

There were significant decreases in the number of ED visits related to three types of infections: tonsillitis (11 percent), viral infections (11 percent), and eye infections (7 percent).

Data Source

The estimates in this Statistical Brief are based upon data from the Healthcare Cost and Utilization Project (HCUP) Nationwide Emergency Department Sample (NEDS), 2006 through 2011. The statistics were generated from HCUPnet, a free, online query system that provides users with *immediate access* to the largest set of publicly available, all-payer national, regional, and State-level hospital care databases from HCUP.[6] Supplemental sources included population denominator data for use with HCUP databases.[7] P-values were computed using a two-sample z-test. Results were considered nominally significant if the value was 0.05 or less.

End Notes

[1] Weiss AJ, Wier LM, Stocks C, Blanchard J. Overview of Emergency Department Visits in the United States, 2011. HCUP Statistical Brief #174. June 2014. Agency for Healthcare Research and Quality, Rockville, MD. http://www.hcupus.ahrq.gov/reports/statbriefs/sb174-Emergency-Department-Visits-Overview.pdf. Accessed August 12, 2014.

[2] Tang N, Stein J, Hsia RY, Maselli JH, Gonzales R. Trends and characteristics of US emergency department visits, 1997–2007. Journal of the American Medical Association. 2010;304:664–70.

[3] Brown RS, Peikes D, Peterson G, Schore J. Six features of Medicare coordinated care demonstration programs that cut hospital admissions of high-risk patients. Health Affairs. 2012;31:1156–66.

[4] Foote S. Population-based disease management under fee-for-service Medicare. Health Affairs. 2003;W3-342-56.

[5] Centers for Disease Control and Prevention. Past Flu Seasons. Last updated July 2014. http://www.cdc.gov/flu/pastseasons/index.htm. Accessed August 12, 2014.

[6] Agency for Healthcare Research and Quality. HCUPnet web site. http://hcupnet.ahrq.gov/. Accessed April 25, 2014.

[7] Barrett M, Lopez-Gonzalez L, Coffey R, Levit K. Population Denominator Data for use with the HCUP Databases (Updated with 2012 Population data). HCUP Methods Series Report #2013-01. Online. March 8, 2013. U.S. Agency for Healthcare Research and Quality. http://www.hcup-us.ahrq.gov/reports/methods/2013 01.pdf. Accessed December 13, 2013.

In: Hospital Emergency Departments
Editor: Daniel T. Lee
ISBN: 978-1-63482-170-4

Chapter 5

REASONS FOR EMERGENCY ROOM USE AMONG U.S. CHILDREN: NATIONAL HEALTH INTERVIEW SURVEY, 2012*

Renee M. Gindi and Lindsey I. Jones

KEY FINDINGS

Data from the National Health Interview Survey, 2012

- In 2012, children with Medicaid coverage were more likely than uninsured children and those with private coverage to have visited the emergency room (ER) at least once in the past year.
- About 75% of children's most recent visits to an ER in the past 12 months took place at night or on a weekend, regardless of health insurance coverage status.
- The seriousness of the medical problem was less likely to be the reason that children with Medicaid visited the ER at their most recent visit compared with children with private insurance.
- Among children whose most recent visit to the ER was for reasons other than the seriousness of the medical problem, the majority visited the ER because the doctor's office was not open.

* This is an edited, reformatted and augmented version of NCHS Data Brief, No. 160, issued by the National Center for Health Statistics, July 2014.

Emergency rooms (ERs) are intended to provide care for acute and life-threatening medical conditions for people of all ages, but use is highest among older adults and young children [1]. In 2012, 18% of children aged 0–17 years visited the ER at least once in the past year [2]. Rising health care costs make it important to understand the reasons that families with children seek ER care, rather than less expensive office-based or outpatient care [3]. Families visiting the ER at night or on weekends may have different characteristics or reasons for using the ER than those who visit during the day [4] Previous research among adults found that the majority visited the ER because “only a hospital could help,” or the “doctor’s office [was] not open” [5] This report provides comparable statistics on reasons for children’s ER use.

Keywords: Health care utilization, health insurance

CHILDREN WITH MEDICAID COVERAGE WERE MORE LIKELY TO HAVE AT LEAST ONE ER VISIT IN THE PAST YEAR, COMPARED WITH THE UNINSURED AND THOSE WITH PRIVATE COVERAGE

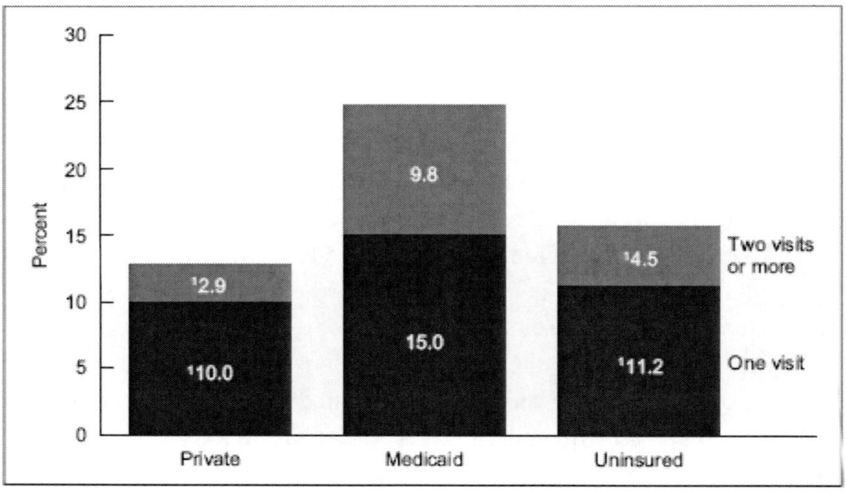

Source: CDC/NCHS, National Health Interview Survey, 2012.
[1]Significantly different from children with Medicaid.

Figure 1. Children aged 0–17 years with at least one emergency room visit in the past 12 months, by health insurance coverage status: United States, 2012.

In 2012, almost one in four children aged 0–17 with Medicaid coverage visited the ER at least once in the past 12 months (24.8%) (Figure 1). This was significantly higher than the percentage of uninsured children (15.7%) and the percentage of children with private insurance (12.9%) who visited the ER at least once in the past 12 months. This relationship was seen for both those visiting the ER only once and those visiting two times or more in the past 12 months.

For Three in Four Children with an ER Visit in the Past 12 Months, the Most Recent Visit Was at Night or on a Weekend, Regardless of Health Insurance Coverage Status

Among children with at least one ER visit in the past 12 months, almost 75% of the most recent ER visits were at night or on a weekend (Figure 2). This percentage was similar for children with private insurance (71.4%), Medicaid (75.4%), and those who were uninsured (75.0%).

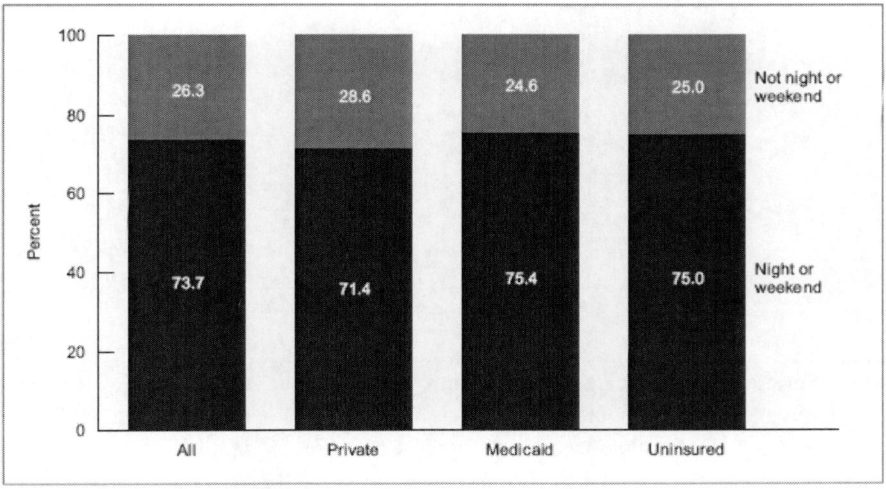

Source: CDC/NCHS, National Health Interview Survey, 2012.

Figure 2. Timing of most recent emergency room visit among children aged 0–17 years with an emergency room visit in the past 12 months, by health insurance coverage status: United States, 2012.

CHILDREN WITH MEDICAID WERE LESS LIKELY THAN CHILDREN WITH PRIVATE INSURANCE TO VISIT THE ER FOR REASONS REFLECTING THE SERIOUSNESS OF THE MEDICAL PROBLEM

Among privately insured children with at least one ER visit in the past 12 months, 67.9% of most recent ER visits were for a reason reflecting the seriousness of the medical problem, compared with 60.6% of children with Medicaid and 59.0% of uninsured children (Figure 3). Children with Medicaid (32.9%) who had at least one ER visit in the past 12 months were more likely than those with private insurance (26.4%) to visit most recently for a reason other than those reflecting the seriousness of the medical problem. No reasons were selected for a smaller percentage of most recent ER visits (6.5%).

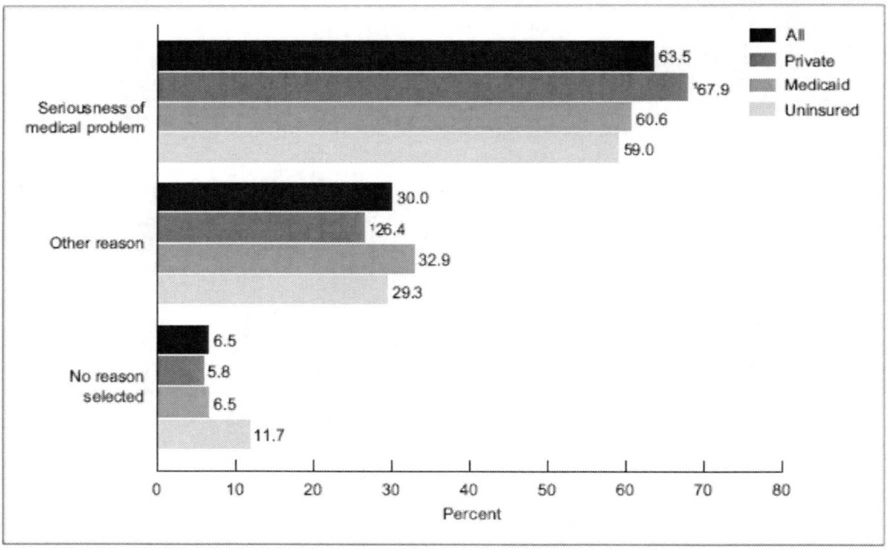

Note: "Seriousness of medical problem" and "Other reason" are summaries based on positive responses to questions about reasons for emergency room visit. For details, see "Definitions" section of report. Categories are mutually exclusive.

Source: CDC/NCHS, National Health Interview Survey, 2012.

[1]Significantly different from children with Medicaid.

Figure 3. Selected reasons for most recent emergency room visit among children aged 0–17 years with an emergency room visit in the past 12 months, by health insurance coverage status: United States, 2012.

AMONG THOSE VISITING THE ER FOR REASONS REFLECTING THE SERIOUSNESS OF THE MEDICAL PROBLEM, THE MOST COMMON REASON WAS THAT ONLY A HOSPITAL COULD HELP

"Only a hospital could help" (79.1%) and "the problem was too serious for a doctor's office" (62.0%) were the most common reasons for the most recent ER visit related to the seriousness of the medical problem among children aged 0–17 who had an ER visit reflecting the seriousness of the medical problem in the past 12 months (Figure 4). Of children who visited the ER for a reason reflecting the seriousness of the medical problem, privately insured children were the most likely to visit the ER because a health provider said to go (43.4%), compared with children with Medicaid (36.3%) and uninsured children (19.5%).

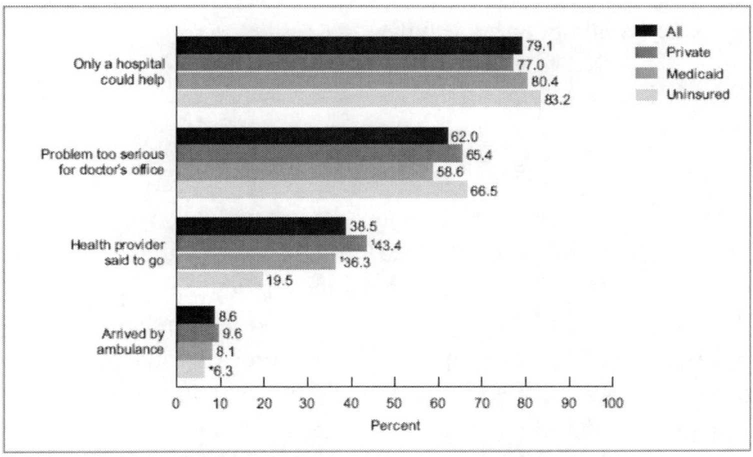

Source: CDC/NCHS, National Health Interview Survey, 2012.

[1]Significantly different from uninsured children.

* Estimate has a relative standard error greater than 30% and less than or equal to 50% and is considered unreliable. Estimate should be used with caution. NOTE: "Seriousness of medical problem" is a summary based on positive responses to any of the related detailed reasons included in this figure. Respondents could select more than one reason.

Figure 4. Selected reasons for most recent emergency room visit among children aged 0–17 years who had an emergency room visit in the past 12 months for a reason reflecting the seriousness of the medical problem, by health insurance coverage status: United States, 2012.

Less than 10% of children's most recent ER visits related to the seriousness of the medical problem were because the child arrived at the ER by ambulance.

Among Children Whose Most Recent ER Visit Was for Reasons Other Than Those Reflecting the Seriousness of the Medical Problem, the Most Common Reason Was Because Their Doctor's Office Was Not Open

Among children aged 0–17 whose most recent visit to the ER in the past 12 months was for a reason other than the seriousness of the medical problem, there were no significant differences in reasons by insurance type (Figure 5). The most common reason for the most recent ER visit was that the "doctor's office [was] not open" (86.0%).

Summary

During 2012, children with Medicaid were more likely to have had at least one ER visit compared with children with private insurance or uninsured children. Approximately 75% of children's most recent ER visits were at night or on the weekend, and this percentage was similar regardless of health insurance coverage status. Approximately two-thirds of children's most recent visits to the ER were due to reasons that reflected the seriousness of the medical problem, and this differed by health insurance coverage status. Children with Medicaid were less likely to visit the ER because of reasons reflecting the seriousness of the medical problem and more likely to visit for other reasons. Similar to adults aged 18–64, common reasons for children's most recent ER visits were because "only a hospital could help" and the "doctor's office [was] not open" [5]. Some reasons for ER visits (e.g., "no other place to go" and "doctor's office [was] not open") may depend on whether a child has a regular source of care, an association seen previously among adults [5]. Recent changes to children's health insurance coverage make it important to monitor the rates, timing, and reasons for ER use by health insurance coverage status.

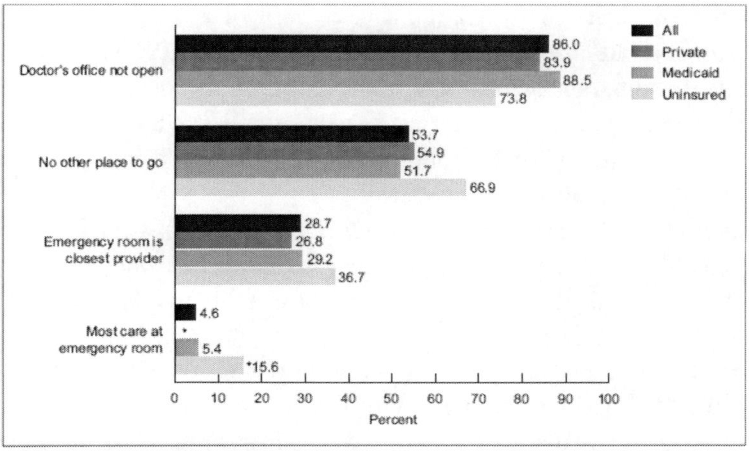

Source: CDC/NCHS, National Health Interview Survey, 2012.

Note: "Reasons other than seriousness of the medical problem" is a summary based on positive responses to any of the related detailed reasons included in this figure. Respondents could select more than one reason.

* Estimate has a relative standard error (RSE) greater than 30% and less than or equal to 50% and is considered unreliable. Estimate should be used with caution. Data not shown have an RSE greater than 50%.

Figure 5. Selected reasons for most recent emergency room visit among children aged 0–17 years whose emergency room visit in the past 12 months was for a reason other than the seriousness of the medical problem, by health insurance coverage status: United States, 2012.

DEFINITIONS

Emergency room visit: Based on the response provided to the question "During the past 12 months, how many times has [sample child] gone to a hospital emergency room about [his/her] health? (This includes emergency room visits that resulted in a hospital admission.)"

Health insurance coverage: The "private insurance coverage" category includes children who had any comprehensive private insurance plan (including health maintenance and preferred provider organizations). These plans include those obtained through an employer, purchased directly, or purchased through local or community programs. Private coverage excludes plans that pay for only one type of service, such as accidents or dental care. The "Medicaid" category includes children without private insurance who reported Medicaid, Children's Health Insurance Program (CHIP), and other state-sponsored health plans. Children were defined as uninsured if they did not have any private insurance, Medicare, Medicaid, CHIP, state-sponsored or other government-sponsored health plan, or military plan at the time of interview. Children also were defined as uninsured if they had only Indian Health Service coverage or had only a private plan that paid for one type of service, such as accidents or dental care.

Reasons for last emergency room visit: Respondents who indicated that the sample child had visited the emergency room at least once in the past 12 months were then asked, "Tell me which of these apply to [sample child's] last emergency room visit? 'you didn't have another place to go,' 'your doctor's office or clinic was not open,' 'your health provider advised you to go,' 'the problem was too serious for the doctor's office or clinic,' 'only a hospital could help you,' 'the emergency room is your closest provider,' 'you get most of your care at the emergency room,' 'you arrived by ambulance or other emergency vehicle.'" Respondents could select more than one reason, and reasons were not mutually exclusive. Three mutually exclusive categories of reasons for last ER visit were developed: children who went to the ER due to reasons reflecting the seriousness of medical problem, those who went for reasons other than the seriousness of the medical problem, and those who did not select any of the reasons listed.

"Seriousness of medical problem" is a summary based on positive responses to any of the following: "your health provider advised you to go," "the problem was too serious for the doctor's office or clinic," "only a hospital could help you," or "you arrived by ambulance or other emergency vehicle." Among children who did not attend the ER for a reason reflecting the seriousness of the medical problem, "Other reason" is a summary based on positive responses to any of the following: "you didn't have another place to go," "your doctor's office or clinic was not open," "the emergency room is your closest provider," or "you get most of your care at the emergency room."

Timing of last emergency room visit: Based on the response provided to the question "Thinking about [sample child's] most recent emergency room visit, did [he/she] go to the emergency room either at night or on the weekend?"

Data Source and Methods

The National Health Interview Survey (NHIS) is a multipurpose health survey conducted continuously throughout the year by the Centers for Disease

Control and Prevention's (CDC) National Center for Health Statistics (NCHS). Interviews are conducted in respondents' homes, but follow-ups to complete interviews may be conducted over the telephone. A sample child is randomly selected from each family in NHIS, and information about the sample child is obtained from an adult residing in the household who is knowledgeable about the child's health (usually the parent). Questions about children's ER use are from the Sample Child Core and Supplemental components of the survey. Questions about health insurance are from the Family Core component. Information was collected for 13,275 children.

Survey design and weighting procedures are described in more detail elsewhere [6]. To account for the complex sample design of NHIS, point estimates and significance tests (using $p < 0.05$) were calculated using SUDAAN software, version 11.0.0 (RTI International, Research Triangle Park, N.C.). The Taylor series linearization method was chosen for variance estimation. All estimates shown in this report meet the NCHS standard of reliability (relative standard error less than or equal to 30%) unless otherwise noted. For further information about NHIS, including the questionnaire, visit the NHIS website: *http://www.cdc.gov/nchs/nhis.htm.*

About the Authors

Renee M. Gindi and Lindsey I. Jones are with CDC's National Center for Health Statistics, Division of Health Interview Statistics.

References

[1] National Center for Health Statistics. Health, United States, 2012: With special feature on emergency care. Hyattsville, MD. 2013.

[2] Bloom B, Jones LI, Freeman G. Summary health statistics for U.S. children: National Health Interview Survey, 2012. National Center for Health Statistics. *Vital Health Stat*. 10(258). 2013.

[3] Machlin SR. Expenses for a hospital emergency room visit, 2003. Rockville, MD: *Agency for Healthcare Research and Quality*. 2006.

[4] Pachter LM, Ludwig S, Groves A. Night people: Utilization of a pediatric emergency department during the late night. *Pediatr. Emerg. Care* 7(1):12–4. 1991.

[5] Gindi RM, Cohen RA, Kirzinger WK. Emergency room use among adults aged 18–64: Early release of estimates from the National Health Interview Survey, January–June 2011. *National Center for Health Statistics*. 2012.

[6] Parsons VL, Moriarity CL, Jonas K, et al. Design and estimation for the National Health Interview Survey, 2006–2015. National Center for Health Statistics. *Vital Health Stat.* 2(165). 2014.

INDEX

A

B

C

D

E

F

L

M

N

O

P

T

U

V

W

X